Applause for
The Hungry Self

"An inspired psychoanalytic meditation on contemporary female identity and eating disorders."
—Phyllis Chesler

"Kim Chernin offers a perspective that is refreshingly different. Her identification of the roots of eating disorders in women's roles is a positive step, and her solution far more joyous than any other I have seen."
—Robin Lakoff, *San Francisco Chronicle*

Praise for
In My Mother's House

"A fascinating, rich, beautiful book. . . . A profound portrayal of the ever-changing, deepening relationship between mother, daughter, and eventually, granddaughter."
—Tillie Olsen

"This brave and thoughtful memoir is an artistic triumph that brings rich characters to life while quickening the feelings that lie at the heart of every family's struggle."
—Helen Mayer, *Newsday*

BOOKS BY KIM CHERNIN

Crossing the Border
The Flame Bearers (A Novel)
The Obsession
The Hungry Self
Reinventing Eve
The Hunger Song (Poetry)
In My Mother's House
Sex and Other Sacred Games (with Renate Stendhal)

A Different Kind of Listening

*My Psychoanalysis
and Its Shadow*

Kim Chernin

HarperPerennial
A Division of HarperCollinsPublishers

First HarperPerennial edition published 1996.

Designed by George J. McKeon

The Library of Congress has catalogued the hardcover edition as follows:

Chernin, Kim.
    A different kind of listening : my psychoanalysis and its shadow / Kim Chernin.
       p.   cm.
    ISBN 0-06-017118-9
    1. Psychoanalysis—Case studies. 2. Chernin, Kim. I. Title.
RC509.8C48   1995
616.89'17—dc20   94-33773

ISBN 0-06-092689-9 (pbk.)

96 97 98 99 00 ❖/RRD 10 9 8 7 6 5 4 3 2 1

For
Otto Allen Will, Jr.
(the old man)
In Memoriam

Contents

Acknowledgments

Renate Stendhal, always my first reader, accurately diagnosed theoretical and textual problems, then marked out a gentle treatment for their cure. Our never-ending conversation has made its way into everything I write.

Cathy Gallagher and I discussed at length every idea in this book. She then peered into the book's shadows, where she discovered both its hidden structure and its name. Through her inspired reading, I have gradually come to understand the meaning of what I have written.

Michael Bader, with whom I have studied and debated psychoanalytic ideas for many years, had an uncanny sensitivity to all those places where I failed to get into language the inner and preverbal states I was trying to describe.

Lisbe Mayer read a late version of the manuscript and drew my attention to narrative implications only a psychoanalyst would notice. Her highly detailed reading has reminded me how closely texts and psychoanalytic conversations resemble each other.

Michael Rogin and I have been conducting our own "shadow analysis" for a long time. His attentive, nuanced reading has helped me distinguish story-telling from what-might-have-happened, a good version from a better one.

Lillian Rubin has been hearing about this book from the moment of its inception on a walk through Chinatown. Our discussions, conversations, clinical talks, and excited voices are the background from which this work has emerged.

I am also grateful to Margot Duxler, Beulah Parker, and Frederick Crews for their reading and critique. Hugh Van Dusen and Diane Cleaver have provided all the care, attention, and support one could possibly wish from editor and agent.

Prologue

An Experiment

I have never yet written a book that worked out the way I planned it. In this respect, a book is similar to a psychoanalysis. For this book about psychoanalysis I have imagined a structure similar to the medieval Russian triptych that stands above my desk. I received it as a gift from a Russian boy over thirty years ago, shortly after I returned from a trip to the (former) Soviet Union. The triptych had been stolen from a church, smuggled out of the Soviet Union, mailed to me from England, along with the advice that I not speak to anyone about its origins. I imagine this precaution is no longer necessary.

The triptych is small, made of enameled brass, although most of the enamel has been worn away. The wings are inserted into four holes carved out of an ornamental loop above and below the central panel. The entire piece can be folded up to lie flat in a traveling bag, in a pocket next to one's hip or against one's heart. I have always carried it with me when I have moved, or gone to stay in a new place for a time. At home, it stands open on a shelf near my writing table, perhaps in the hope that its long, complex history will preside over my work. A stolen icon, its imagery worn away, but still decipherable here and there, it reminds me of memory itself, which also has its stolen, transgressive quality, having come into existence by robbing time of its full share of what otherwise, apart from memory, would simply have been swept away.

In the central panel of the icon there is a madonna, with heavy-lidded, closed eyes, a broad Slavic nose, high cheekbones in an oval face, a worn mouth that might be creased in adoration of the small robed figure standing in front of her, not quite in her arms, a bushy-haired, face-less baby Christ, with one finger raised, close to the mother's chin, as if to demonstrate an obscure, essential point or deliver a blessing. They are surrounded by a Byzantine coil of flowers set in an almost vanished blue enamel, although the halo that encloses both of them has a good covering of white. This worn, chipped, defaced, treasured icon also reminds me of memory for precisely these qualities. Above the mother and child, in an onion dome cut from the same piece of brass, there is a worn figure with extended arms or wings, a god or holy ghost perhaps, poised above a ropelike knot of clouds to indicate the heavens. But the wings of the triptych, which have three inset panels each, are sufficiently worn to make it difficult to say with any precision just what scenes in the story of Christ they represent. Sometimes, on the left, I think I can make out a weary donkey with its head bowed. Below it, I used to see a bell or a well from which a tree seemed to be growing, although this might be a manger with the smudged brass figures next to it kneeling in adoration. From an exhausted curve on the facing wing I imagine Christ carrying his cross, but if I did not already know this story I would have to content myself with speculations, although in the box below there seem to be angels and in the gathered crowd a gesture reminiscent of prayer. This hazardous, speculative, informed, highly inflected reading of the icon reminds me of the sort of reconstructive memory work that goes on in psychoanalysis, in which you can make a story out of the merest traces, especially if you already have a good idea of what that story is.

Probably because of the mother and child in the central panel, and because the mother is by far the best-preserved figure in the icon, as well as the largest, this triptych has come to mind as I sit down to begin my book. While everything else remains a conjecture, the clouds, the god or holy ghost, the donkey, the suffering Christ of the cross, the gesture of prayer, the manger or bell, there can be no doubt about the identity of the mother and child. About their centrality the icon, like memory itself, seems to have no hesitation. Time has not been allowed to carry out any confusions here.

There are also of course the inevitable incongruities. I

am a Jewish woman who, for the last thirty years, has been carrying a Christian icon around with her all over the world. When I first received it, I was unimpressed by the story of Christ, ignorant of the triptych's symbolism. I liked it because it had been stolen. I treasured the icon because it was a gift of love, or more precisely, a gift of sexual attraction. That psychoanalysis does not think highly of religion adds to these incongruities. Psychoanalysis, when thought of as a science, would see itself as antithetical to my little icon with its mysterious evocations. Nevertheless, every time I sit down to take notes for my book, even when I am sitting on a park bench or in a café, the little icon comes to mind. I can see the whole thing quite clearly just before I begin to write. It cannot be shaken as the presiding image for the structure of my book, which is evidently imagined to take place in three parts, each complete in itself but legitimately connected to the others by means of a common theme.

On the other hand, the idea of three parts is dangerous. Each might develop into a book in its own right, the three parts breaking off from one another to expand illegitimately into a trilogy. That's happened to me before; it might be inevitable. Still, during this first, audacious phase, filled with what many psychoanalytic practitioners would regard as self-inflation, grandiosity, narcissism, I imagine that I shall compose a triptych on the subject of psychoanalysis itself. In the left wing I will set down everything I can remember about the twenty-five years I spent in analytic therapy, the illuminations along with the shadows: a solid twenty-five years, with a break of no more than eight or nine months during most of which I lived in Israel.

To compose this wing of my book I imagine a discipline similar to psychoanalysis itself. Every day, at a certain time, I will sit myself down in front of my computer, to transcribe whatever comes to mind, precisely as it occurs to me. The only restriction I will impose upon myself is that my writing keep track of the years I spent on the couch. If all goes well, this exercise will become a lengthy, written free association on a set theme.

When I first went into psychoanalysis, in 1967, the childhood I was then attempting to remember was closer to me than my beginning as a psychoanalytic patient is now. To write about the years I spent in psychoanalysis, I have to undertake the same remembering I experienced during the analysis itself. I find this fascinating, perhaps impossible. But that is how I like to imagine it, in this first glorious phase when anything seems possible.

At the center of my composition, if I get that far, I will inscribe something about my work with the psychoanalytic teacher I met during my transition from psychoanalytic patient to psychoanalytic lay practitioner. From him, over many years, I gradually learned how to undo everything I had been learning over the years I had been engaged in psychoanalysis. Because my teacher was a practitioner of the ancient art of storytelling, teaching by precept and parable, wit and humor, rather than by theory, I, in homage to him, and to render accurately what I learned from him, will spin a yarn about our work together, the friendship that evolved from it, the profound unlearning it evolved, to bring me at last to a state in which, emerging from shadow, I began to listen to my clients, I think it would be true to say: for the first time.

If these two panels remain within the triptych, if they don't break apart into the trilogy they might become, in the right wing I will set down what I have begun to hear through this different kind of listening. The hearing that allows another person to develop her unique voice is a strange business. It requires a capacity for spontaneous self-expression on the listener's part, while simultaneously asking for surrender to the storyteller's imperative need to shape the ideal listener. All this is, of course, very different from the cooler, more traditional psychoanalytic listening I had come to know during my own twenty-five analytic years.

Then, I will have ended my book. I will get to write an epilogue. An epilogue, of course, is the point of the whole thing. Structurally, it is reminiscent of that onion dome with its pontificating god or holy ghost. For, if you have had the stamina to get through an entire creation, you deserve to make some claim for your own originality. In my case, keeping in mind the hours I have spent debating whether psychoanalysis is a science or an art, I will suggest (I will certainly not set forth, establish beyond doubt, declare, demonstrate, much less prove) that psychoanalysis is a continually evolving ritual, or better yet, a noble game, in which the rules must remain unknown to the participants until they have evolved between them, and even then are continually changing, so that when finally learned, the analysis may be said to be at an end.

But to justify this claim I had first better write a book.

Let's take stock. The plans have been laid, a three-part structure has been announced, a transformational excursion has been foreseen, during which the psychoanalytic patient (Kim Chernin) will be transformed into a psychoanalytic listener. If I actually succeed in carrying out this plan, it is the reader, for whom these memories and speculations and stories are being assembled, who will be left to form a sense of the pattern among the random things that emerge, helter skelter, from the charnel house of memory.

But of course this is inevitable. If I try to write this book in a way that suggests the psychoanalytic process itself, aiming for a free association, but subject of course to the familiar obstacles, resistances, hesitations, diversions, the writer will have been given the role of analysand, the reader will be expected to become the silent analyst, while the subject of memory will be psychoanalysis itself. Not that a book can possibly remain as free, unpremeditated, wild, rough, crude, and halting as the verbal free association by which analytic work proceeds. Before I let this manuscript out into the public I will have scratched out, written over, revised, edited, torn up, and thrown away material that might prove the most salacious and revealing if only it were left in place. But I shall mark its traces, leaving behind the fossil prints of what has vanished from the text as I assemble the fragments of memory that have endured against that forgetting which is the enemy of literary, as well as psychoanalytic, work. Which work, as it happens, I began one day in March or April during a time of considerable turmoil, in my twenty-sixth year, almost thirty years ago now.

No, I cannot begin where I had thought to begin. From the moment I assigned a beginning (1967) to my psychoanalytic tale, a memory of an aborted attempt to begin psychoanalysis intruded. This intrusion of memory, which is the point of psychoanalytic work, plays havoc with writing. Schemes, plans, parts, forms, sequences of chapters are immediately rendered suspect, along with the notes one has been writing down, the effaced memory traces one has been researching. Even the beginning is not where one imagined it to be, but further off, back beyond the orderly memory patch one had plowed. It is the sudden, violent nature of these intrusions that makes one dread the empty page, and this is the same dread I have always felt on my way to a psychoanalytic session. Because of this dread, I suspect, many people gifted with language do not become writers. As for me, to make sure that I got to my psychoanalytic sessions on time, I have always provided a good half hour or more beyond what is needed. I have always known that I would contrive obstacles, of the same kind that keep me from getting down to work every morning at the break of dawn, although I am disciplined, establish a routine, stick to it as far as possible. Small things. The drawerful of socks that need folding before one can get dressed. A coffeepot that has to be rinsed with baking soda before making the coffee. There is a conspicuous dread at work behind these maneuvers, a wish to take to one's heels before facing the unknown. If there is a better or worse way to get to my psychoanalytic session, I will infallibly select the route with a traffic jam, an accident, a broken water main, arriving on time only because of the extra time I have allowed. Over the years, I have become an expert calculator of these detours, which psychoanalysis would call resistance. I have also tried to get myself on their side. They do, after all, express one's legitimate protest against the task of recollection. If I have to suddenly clean out the broom closet before sitting down at my desk, or search for my keys before starting out on the long drive to my analyst's office, honor must be accorded these evasive measures. To them I give an assigned place in my schedule.

For example, this rumination on evasions should

undoubtedly be regarded as an evasion itself, for the way it has interposed itself between that memory I mentioned and my written account of it here. I mean the memory of my aborted attempt to begin psychoanalysis, which throws the beginning of my psychoanalytic work back some six, even seven years to the fall of 1960. That was when I was living in Oxford with my husband, who was a graduate student of philosophy at University College. I too attended lectures and met with a tutor, but I was registered with the university as an "extraordinary student," which meant I was not formally enrolled. I was twenty years old, I had begun to write poetry, I liked to walk along the river to recite it to myself, while I wept and felt desperate. Desperate enough finally, whatever that meant at the time, to make regular appointments, four times a week, for psychoanalytic sessions in London. Although I had asked around, as discreetly as possible, there did not seem to be psychoanalysts practicing at that time in Oxford.

This is what I had to do to start psychoanalysis.

I had to leave Oxford by bus during the early afternoon in order to arrive on time for a late-evening session. Before the session, I had to check in at the youth hostel, where I would spend the night in order to attend a session early the next morning. Then I would return to Oxford by bus, spend a day or two at lectures, get on the bus again one early afternoon that week, to check in at the youth hostel, take the underground and two buses to my analyst's house in the suburbs, return to the dormitory room at the hostel, where it was very cold, and where I could not use an alarm clock to wake up on time for my next morning's early session, which took place during the first twilight of an English morning I found consistently heartless.

These details matter. Now that they have returned, I understand the reason for their persistence. In no other way could I measure the degree to which I felt miserable in those days. Left to myself, without the insistence of this memory, I would be inclined to cast myself as the sensitive, troubled young poet, approach the figure with irony, wave her back into a well-deserved insignificance. I would not be able to take her seriously because there is something about her suffering that disturbs me to this day.

The suffering of the young girl in Oxford. I would now call it pre-psychoanalytic, because little by little it took itself off during my psychoanalytic years, to be replaced by other sorts of sorrows, which had become, however, essentially different, because I had begun to name them. That older, nameless suffering is like nothing else in this world, although I imagine many people spend most of their lives evading it. The suffering makes no sense, it does not match up with one's life circumstances, it does not seem to derive from those circumstances. A young marriage with its promise of a lifetime together. Money enough to spend years in Europe studying, eventually to afford a small car. A brilliant husband, who also happened to be a dark-eyed, dreamy-looking man. A good head on my own shoulders. The poetry that came and went but always came back again. A pretty face, a winning way with people.

Anyone who feels desperate in these conditions will have to despise herself. I did. I knew that I was privileged, should be happy, but found my life unbearable at times, to the point of wishing to be dead.

Wishing to be dead while having every reason to live is a peculiar sort of distress. I knew no one else like me, at that time before anyone I knew had begun to talk freely about psychological difficulties. I did not believe in psychological difficulties. If one of the *clochards* I had seen sleeping on the hot-air vents in Paris, during the early fall days before we arrived in Oxford, had jumped to his feet, run wildly down the street to throw himself into the Seine, I could have understood that. But why had the thought occurred to me, walking along the quais with a tattered copy of Proust in my hands, just purchased from the old book vendor?

I have to hold that young woman steady before my gaze, reading her the way I read the icon, with its suggestive obscurities. What I can understand about her now will probably have to be leached out of those bus rides from Oxford to London, from the youth hostel to the suburbs. She hated them. She was always afraid of getting lost. She didn't know how to read the underground maps. She was forever getting on the wrong train, so that she had to get off (she was often inexplicably, suddenly very shy) to ask directions of strangers. It was hard for her to wake up without an alarm clock in the dank, huge dormitory, in which two or three other people were sleeping, none of whom ever spoke to her. The English money confused her. The people who waited in orderly queues for the buses did not seem to mind the cold, the drizzle, the overcast, the murky early-morning light. If I keep her steady in my gaze, I see that she has not yet bought a coat warm enough for the climate. Her feet are wet. Other people are wearing galoshes. She's afraid to be late for her appointment. This makes the bus take for-ever. She has no idea where she is going. How will she know where to get off? If I stick with her, leaving aside the question of whether she deserves to feel desperate enough not to want to go on living, I come smack up against her dilemma. She would do anything, go through anything, endure whatever has to be endured, to want to go on living. Therefore, what we think of as the life force must be very powerful in her. This life force has brought her up to London under these difficult conditions, to begin a process of self-examination of which her parents (Marxists) would not approve. She has come up to Lon-don in preference to letting herself leap from a bridge, throw herself in front of the bus. For her, the wish to die is the known. She does not know it is the wish to live that even now is giving her a hand up into the bus, to ask the driver to call out her stop, while everyone is looking at her, probably because of her American accent, or because her hair has begun to curl in the drizzle that has just turned into a heavy rain. Of course, she does not have an umbrella.

Things are going better than I would have expected. Beyond a word or two, I haven't had to scrap anything yet. The written record is (so far) keeping track of a spontaneous movement of thought. I made only one change. I went back to my first section to describe the icon in greater detail. This seems to have been a good move. The icon led to the girl in the rain at the London bus stop. This girl holds the aborted memory of my first attempt at psychoanalysis, when I was twenty years old.

The girl in the rain has also led to some interesting questions that would never otherwise have occurred to me. In that sense, as it moves from image to memory to curiosity, the writing is behaving psychoanalytically. It goes along in its seemingly lawless way, jumping from Byzantine icon to girl in the rain.

If I were to reason psychoanalytically about this move, I might ask: Is it the icon's image of mother and child that has led to the lost girl who wants to die? Perhaps the lost girl is grieving a troubled relationship with her own mother? Or maybe the lost girl is close enough in time to the younger girl who received the icon to stand in for her? Only two or three years separate the two. Holding them up next to each other, memory image to memory image, I can scarcely believe they are the same person. The younger girl, who had gone to the Soviet Union, was a voluptuous seventeen-year-old, out into the world for the first time, wide-eyed, streetwise, desperately romantic, tough, exuberant. She wore tight black turtleneck sweaters, seemed always to be in a pout, had nothing in mind but attracting men, could stay up all night waiting for a boat or a train, enthusiastically eat cold spaghetti for breakfast. On the student boat taking her to Europe to attend the Youth Festival in Moscow, three men from Harvard fell in love with her. She fell for the German crew hand who had smuggled himself off a boat in America, got caught, was working his way back to Europe on another boat. The German boy, who was lithe, dark-haired, looked Italian, gave her a medal to wear when they had to separate at Le Havre. She wore it until the next boy asked for it, giving her a medal of his own in exchange. What else can be said about her? She wore her hair short, had a fierce, stubborn, rebellious look to her, as of someone who has fallen too soon from the nest but comes down fighting.

Between her and the lost girl in the rain there would seem to be nothing in common. The three years that separate them have changed their looks dramatically. The girl getting out of bed in the youth hostel, slipping out of her nightshirt to get dressed, is very thin. This may be one of the reasons she is on her way to a psychoanalyst.

She is very unhappy, but she does not know why. Compared to the girl who received the Byzantine icon, she looks strangely withered, as if she had been at pains to efface all signs of youth and beauty. Her cheeks are hollow, there are dark circles under her eyes. She does not wear makeup, ties her hair back in a ponytail or bun, her eyes look too large for the slender face, the head a bit too big for the emaciated body. Two, three years later, the girl who had gone charging out into life to fall in love with every handsome boy has become rather nunlike, as if she were retreating in terror from her own exuberance, the heady pleasure of getting away from the family for the first time, making her own decisions, eating spaghetti for breakfast, dancing all night on a deserted quai in Belgium with a boy from South Africa, who speaks Afrikaans.

The story that connects these two young women must be a fascinating tale, but I don't know it. The girl at the bus stop feels no sense of connection to the girl receiving the icon in the mail. She isn't curious about her, doesn't wonder what happened to her, has no active memory of her, is not aware that in her various acts of self-starvation she might be trying to starve her out. Anything said about the relationship between the young woman of seventeen (pouting, turtlenecked) and the older woman of twenty (gaunt, nunnish) would have to be speculative, hypothetical, an interpretation.

This is the sort of explanation the young woman

walking through the rain to her analyst's house might
hope to find in psychoanalysis. She might even hope to
find out why she is unhappy. But this girl with wet feet,
who hasn't lived here long enough to know when to
carry an umbrella, has no hopes to speak of, she has no
idea why she is trudging along trying to read the directions on the back of a wet envelope. She couldn't be said
to regret the passing of that younger self, who is said to
have slept not much more than a dozen hours during the
whole ten days she was in Moscow. Probably she has
come up to London because she believes she is not slender enough and cannot control inexplicable, sudden,
episodes of eating. And then, of course, there is that persistent feeling of wanting to die.

Walking up the drive to her analyst's house (memory
says: a stately house), she is, apart from the wish to
starve herself and to die, a patchwork person with no
compelling, central design to her. If all goes well, when
she enters this house, she may become aware of this condition.

Unfortunately, everything goes wrong. She doesn't
like the large, cool, forbidding woman who answers
the door. She feels foolish when she has said hello and
the psychoanalyst hasn't answered. She doesn't know
what to do with her smile, an awkward survivor of their
shipwrecked greeting. This smile lights up her face,
therefore makes her look younger, less exhausted. She is

led to a large room with a couch, a gesture from the analyst suggests she should lie down on the couch, the analyst takes a place behind her in a chair, there is silence.

For some reason our girl blurts out into the silence everything she can remember about her sister's death. It took place when she was four and a half years old. Remembering her sister's death is her first psychoanalytic act. The analyst makes no comment. This gives the girl the impression she is talking about the wrong thing. Still, having started, she finds that she cannot stop herself. She has never before, in any detail, told anyone about her sister's death. Probably the analyst is not aware of this. Perhaps it seems to her that her patient is reciting a well-worn story. Our girl is a talker; she avoids the vernacular. There is probably, in spite of the flow and pressure of words, something stilted in her self-expression, as if she had been rehearsing for the occasion. She worries about grammar, having been taught English by an immigrant mother who cared about such things. No doubt all this does not make a good impression. The analyst says nothing until it is time to inform the girl from Oxford, who has just made it here through the rain and is presently worried about having left watermarks on the analytic couch, that it is time to stop.

Nevertheless, the trip from Oxford, across London, back across London to spend the night in the youth hostel, is repeated. The ordeal lasts three weeks, during which the analyst has not said anything. Then something momentous happens. During the twelfth session, the girl runs out of memories about her sister. The flood of unbearable recollection is over, the emptiness that fills her is now of a different kind, there is a suspicion of relief in it. Should she tell the analyst about this? But the analyst says: "I noticed that you came late to our session this morning."

To the girl, this means she has done something wrong. Doesn't the analyst know about the trip up from Oxford, the dreary youth hostel, the having to get up without an alarm clock, the confusion of the under-ground, the inability to read the maps, the wet trip across London to the suburbs, where all the houses and all the streets look the same, so that she, who does not have a sense of direction, needs to keep following the crumpled directions on the handwritten map she is terrified to lose, because she would be ashamed to ask for new directions, thereby admitting she has still not managed to learn the way? Probably the analyst has not considered these things. She is aware, it seems, of her patient's resistance to being there, not what she has already gone through to get there.

The patient says: "I came late. That's true, I came late. But it wasn't very late, was it? I mean, I think it was only about five minutes late, because the bus didn't arrive on time, or rather, that is, at first I was waiting at the wrong bus stop, then I figured it out because I saw the right bus coming so I ran over there, but I missed it. Not that I'm trying to say five minutes isn't a lot of time to be late. Or that I couldn't have remembered the right bus stop. I have been coming here for three weeks. So you might expect I would know which bus stop . . ."

It seems clear to me that this girl feels criticized. Undoubtedly she is one of those young people highly sensitive to criticism, probably because she's met a great deal of it in her life and maybe even from her mother. If I were her analyst I would regard this sensitivity as crucial information about her. I'd keep away from comments that might sound critical. Of course, I have no idea what that analyst was thinking. I wouldn't want to appear to be judging her after all this time. No doubt she was simply behaving as she'd been taught, with a detached, neutral attitude, diligently commenting on resistance.

Now she has just said, "Our time is over."

The girl leaves the house.

That is the end of her first psychoanalysis.

Memory is above all parsimonious. It seems to have figured out the human capacity for storing things away is extremely limited, will run out one day, had better not be overburdened. Therefore, memory has arranged to record the large and small events of life through details that seem inconsequential and irrelevant, except for the fact that memory has held on to them. After you have been hanging around with psychoanalysis for a time, you develop an enormous respect for scraps, spare parts, fragments. It is through these that memory accomplishes its works of preservation. This appreciation of memory is to my mind, even more than the idea of the unconscious and the mechanism of repression, the single greatest accomplishment of psychoanalysis.

The icon, the seventeen-year-old girl in the black turtleneck sweater, the girl in the rain. Taken together, they sketch out a life story. From each of these memory scraps one could elaborate a book-length tale. I could tell scabrous tales about that seventeen-year-old girl. There would also, I am sure, be a lot more to say about the girl who never went back to the analyst in London, didn't call to cancel her next appointment, didn't (ever) pay her bill. To the extent that I feel a connection with the girl in the rain, I am still implicated in her act of protest against psychoanalysis. (Whether or not I feel this connection is a relevant subject for investigation. If I take up this subject here it will lead heaven knows where. Therefore, I will mark the query and, for now, avoid it . . .)

But if I do feel this connection to the girl in the rain I could be said to owe a debt of some twenty-five English pounds to psychoanalysis. Or perhaps I have paid this debt in the way I have always returned a greeting for a greeting, smile for a smile, whenever I have gone out to meet a client for the first time?

Here, of course, I am getting ahead of myself, I could wander off down dangerous passages. Free association and writing are, to this extent, clearly at war with one another, the written task requiring order and coherence, some perceptible indication of form, the presence of an intellect ordering the rapid outpouring of ideas, memories, thoughts, feelings. Meanwhile, the impulse toward wildly flowing ideas is tugging off in a hundred directions, wanting its head, willing to set off on an unchecked gallop through woods, swamp, desert . . .

Now watch this conflict. Against this inclination to muse about my connection to the lost girl, or to charge ahead into the psychoanalytic musings that will form the final section of this book, I feel a stubborn willfulness about sticking with the sequence that has, with fits and starts, more or less consistently unraveled in the direction of the psychoanalytic treatment I began in 1967, which went on, with three different analysts, with several dramatic endings and beginnings, for the next twenty-five years.

On the other hand, how can it hurt to muse a bit? If I want the act of writing to reflect the analytic process, I have to allow the written record to keep track of the mind's spontaneous movements. Beginnings can always be delayed. Getting to them is sometimes half the point of a good story. Once you arrive at a beginning, you already have to face the inevitability of an end, a thought as disturbing in relation to a book as it is with regard to the ending of a psychoanalysis, even though the whole point of undertaking either book or psychoanalysis is to bring it to a fully legitimate close.

Can I say with certainty these possible directions of thought that have arisen, against the direction I had set out for myself, are detours, divergencies, resistances to the task I originally set? Or are they perhaps the point of the whole thing, the secret intention hidden beneath the conscious task? This is the sort of question psychoanalysis may legitimately ask. Let's say, for instance, a patient is talking. As the listener, you have formed an idea of what has been troubling the patient, you keep watch over the stream of associations to detect anything that might keep the patient from getting to the heart of things. But are you right? Have you formed the correct idea about what is troubling the patient? Maybe these verbal flights that seem detours to the analytic listener (as this writing is beginning to seem to me) are in fact on the way to the essential, unguessed core of what really matters? And if this is true, shouldn't I as a writer about psychoanalysis just give the impulse free rein, hang on as best I can, through whatever savage terrain it takes me?

But here an internal check has taken place. I've suddenly grown tired of this wild stuff; it has begun to exhaust me. The orderly world of images has begun to appeal to me again. If I sit here silently, closing my eyes to avoid the urgent blinking of the computer screen, I find myself settling back into a more contemplative mode. Taking stock. Going over the ground covered so far.

The need for order has arisen spontaneously in

response to the wildness that threatens to take over every writing project in which I've been involved. This ordering imperative may be coercive, it may exercise a severe censorship over spontaneous wildness, it probably represents an escape into coherence when the truth may well lie in the surrender to fragmentation. But I need the reassurance of a form, diligently maintained.

If I now developed an extremely sober tone or rigid formal structure, I could be said to have made my way into the literary equivalent of what psychoanalysis calls a "reaction formation," having ended up a formalist when I was about to become a raider of the inarticulate.

I will now return forcibly to my original design.

Icon. Turtleneck sweater. Girl in the rain. These have become the incantations through which the process of free association is guided back into a composed channel. From here on, for as long as I can maintain the discipline, the associations can move freely, in the sense of leading from one thing to another, but they must now follow a set theme. This is the compromise I have reached between the wish to rave and the desire to shape that raving as a meaningful communication. Hovering here at this decisive moment, I am probably choosing between writing and madness.

This choice, it could be noted, has arisen from the type of conflict with which psychoanalysis concerns itself. Whatever story we tell about the wish to grow wild and surrender to impulse, whether we call it a drive, an instinct, an innate biological endowment, or regard it instead as behavior learned from a particular family, most schools of psychoanalysis would recognize the importance of the conflict between wildness and order and allow room for the struggle at center stage. Therefore, if my writing is meant to reflect the surges and retreats of the mind during a psychoanalytic session, I must give this struggle a place on my page.

Okay, let that be my explanation for this unruly section that imagined it would plod right on to a preordained beginning.

One

The First Analysis

(1967–1971)

The woman who went into psychoanalysis in 1967 was in bad shape. Because she is not a person to whom I feel any immediate connection, I can speak about her bluntly. She still thinks about killing herself. She has begun to take measures toward this end. She has saved up the entire collection of drug-company samples that were sent to her husband when he was in medical school. He thinks they have been thrown out; she has meticulously gathered them in from the garbage.

She has read Proust. She has written a novel about growing up in a Communist family. No one wants to publish this novel. She has separated from her husband. That was after they returned to California, where he finished the medical studies he had begun in Dublin, when he gave up philosophy after they moved from Oxford. She, having studied in Weimar, Oxford, Dublin, Los

3

Angeles, has now graduated from the University of California in Berkeley with a degree in English. She has started graduate school. Recently, she had fallen in love with a therapist who had a small institute in Fairfax, out on the road that runs between the town and Bolinas. She had an affair with him. Several times it seemed he was about to leave his wife, but then he didn't.

She also had several years of therapy in Dublin, during a period when she seemed to be running wild, having affairs, taking up with strangers. This therapy, which took place across the street from a large mental hospital in Dublin, led to a decision to stay with her marriage and have a child. Although the marriage broke up a few years later anyway, having the child has been good for her. When, during the night, this would-be mother thinks about the pills stored away in the cellar, the child's presence makes this thought impossible.

She, who is about to begin a process of self-reflection that will last for twenty-five years, has been given a list of the top ten psychoanalysts in San Francisco. She received it from a man she had been dating (he is a psychiatric resident and a well-known jazz musician) since the affair with her therapist in Fairfax came to an end. She called the first two names on the list. She was given the first appointment by the man in second place. She is lucky things have worked out this way. The man whose name came first on the list will commit suicide a few years from now. If she had been in analysis with this man, the suicide from which she had always been running would have caught up with her.

These things do not interest me. They could have happened to anyone.

I don't know exactly what that twenty-six-year-old version of myself looked like. In the few pictures that have lasted since that time, she certainly was not any longer a nun. Most of the time she wears short dresses, shoes with small heels. I have seen her in earrings and tight knit suits, as if she is trying to look respectable but can't keep herself from looking a slut. At the same time, there is something deliberately intellectual about her, a tendency to frown, to look serious when she wants to laugh, to carry her eyes wide open, as if they were meditating invisible matters. She is always carrying a book around with her; worse yet, she is always reading it. Somehow or other she has acquired a hunger for culture. Who is to say if this hunger is real? I myself would not like to suddenly find myself back in her shoes. She's made up of fragments, nothing has come together for her yet, tomorrow she might wake up an entirely different person, having been reorganized by a dream or sudden thought during the night. She might even wake up looking so odd that her next-door neighbor might not recognize her, running down the stairs in a tie-dye shirt, barefoot, or in a pair of old sandals.

To take one example among many: One day, early on a Friday morning, a few months before the psychoanalysis in 1967 begins, her daughter has gone down to Los Angeles to visit her grandparents. Suddenly liberated, the mother jumps in her car, stops to buy bagels on Geary, drives without stopping up to Mendocino, where she has never been before. Straightaway she drives out to the headland, where she gets out of the car for a look, sees a good-looking man with black hair. He is pacing about, with a book in his hand, memorizing his lines in a play. Half an hour later, I mean half an hour later, they are walking together through the long grass on the outskirts of town, up above the ocean, where whales have been sighted. The grass is so high they can sink down into it and make love and no one will be the wiser. She, of course, regards this as precisely the adventure for which she had set out impulsively in the morning. And why not? The man has clearly fallen for her. She spends the weekend with him, attends the rehearsals of *The Glass Menagerie*, in which he is playing the part of the young man who comes to dinner. She makes friends, gives advice about the play, is invited to return. She too can live in the community of artists in the soon-to-be-ruined town, but now still unpainted, weathering, windswept, with a good primary school for her daughter.

Before the weekend is over she has decided to rent her house, pack up her belongings, throw her daughter's clothes into the car, move up the coast. Her new friends up there are looking for jobs for her; she's already been offered something temporary in a bookstore. The young man, whose name is Pavel, has offered her a bed in his place. A group of new friends see her off at the edge of town; she will be back the next weekend. Pavel leans in through the window to kiss her good-bye and never hears from her again!

The next week she mostly stays in bed, feeling strangely let down after the glorious weekend. She manages to get her daughter off to nursery school, but the lunch is not quite all that it should be. The mother has run out of plastic bags, wraps the sandwich in an old bread wrapper. This embarrasses the daughter, the only girl in her class whose carrots are not peeled or sliced in slivers.

In the panhandle of Golden Gate Park, a few blocks from her house on Stanyan Street, she goes down to dance to the rock bands on Sundays. The neighbors complain about the noise, but no one who is stretched out naked on the grass, or climbing the trees, or weaving garlands of flowers, or passing out hash brownies finds the music very loud.

That's what I mean by fragments. The following Wednesday she will spend the entire day in the stacks in Moffatt Library on the Berkeley campus, from the time she drops her daughter off at school. Most people in those days didn't clatter down the spiral stairs or dash out of the stacks and pound their way across the reading room on the second floor.

She doesn't make as tidy a figure as the girl in the

rain. She does not have the tough innocence of the girl in the turtleneck sweater. She wears her hair parted on the side, combed down over her forehead in a gesture at style. Just now, I catch her in a characteristic moment, running because she is late to pick up her daughter. Let's freeze the image. She is overexcited by a day of abstract thought. There is a bead of sweat on her upper lip; no one would believe this woman is a mother. If she doesn't stop soon, at any moment she is going to splinter. That's who she was then. Who knows who will wake up in her bed tomorrow?

If I were speaking to a psychoanalyst now, she would probably comment on my tone of voice. She would have detected an emerging dryness, a tendency to thin out as it reaches its upper register. If she were a very good analyst she would be able to make this comment without suggesting a judgment. For the sake of argument, let us agree. She is not critical. The tone of voice is merely something she has observed. No doubt every time I talk about myself as a young woman there will be an emerging dryness in my tone. She will be able to make her observation again. I probably will not pick up on it, and then one day I probably will. That will serve as a sign that I am ready to consider the meaning of voice tonalities.

It might also mean that the sheer force of repetition has finally made me aware the psychoanalyst wants me to notice something. Therefore, even the most apparently neutral comment, under pressure of repetition, will acquire a communicative power that is perhaps incompatible with the very idea of neutrality. But this is a thought I cannot afford to follow out here. It contains some rancor, a polemical drift, that would be of little interest to anyone not engaged in the inner (some would say sterile) debates about psychoanalytic technique.

Because I spent twenty-five years in psychoanalysis, I have acquired the habit of observing myself the way my analysts might. This is undoubtedly a useful acquisition for someone who used to be impulsive, moody, change-able, unpredictable, supremely unreliable. (Unless one happens to believe in uninhibited impulsivity? Well, let's remember: one can also do away with oneself in an impulsive act.)

I have observed a change in the tone of my writing. This change (dryness, thinness) probably means I am about to repeat some established attitude I have evolved toward myself. Something about the ironic detachment with which I present my younger, troubled self has begun to sound overdone. The point has been made. I, the writer, cannot find a way to connect myself to the person about whom I am writing. If I stick with this idea, I should have something to say with it. Do I? Or am I just trading on a well-worked technique? Is there a legitimate new thought held at bay by the ironic stance I have adopted?

What would it be? Something about the sequence of provisional selves through which we pass in the course of our lives, each self lived for its season, then sloughed off, leaving behind fossil traces (memory), but no immediate, felt sense of the living being who once occupied one's life.

This sense of fragmentation, this discontinuity, may or may not be a condition peculiar to me. It may be the reason my twenty-six-year-old-self is on her way to meet a psychoanalyst. (She has got out of the car, walked up the street a few blocks, has turned back, checked her watch, doesn't want to arrive too early, is sitting in the car again, listening to the classical-music station, wondering if the music is so loud the new analyst might overhear it. If he can, he will know she is a serious person who listens to good music. On the other hand, he might wonder why she has to do everything in a way that calls attention to herself. She turns the radio down.) This provisionality of the self, this explanation for my younger self's persistent distress, has just occurred to me. I count this as a substantial result of writing about myself in the third person. My experiment, some twenty-five years after that day in April 1967, when the young woman is walking in a (hopefully) dignified manner across the street, has yielded at least one potential insight. She, for her part, would be trying to pretend she is not imagining the analyst is looking at her from the curtained window on the second floor of the sprawling house, which must have a spectacular view of the ocean, is situated near the sea, below the golf course. That house, which will shortly become the dream site of assignations, has arched windows, in one of which there is a white Indian antique elephant, head lifted, almost prancing.

This nervous, young, fidgety woman from back then, is pacing about in the small waiting room, to which you gain entrance by ringing the lowest of three doorbells. The upper doorbell signals another analyst, who rents an office on the top floor of the house. It is this analyst who displays the antique elephant that, nevertheless, will always hold for her the tense memory of the man she is about to meet, who will change her life. Soon, it will be every elephant, every Indian elephant, every Indian antique, every sculpted animal, whether or not an elephant, that will, by a process of association familiar to analytic work, have come to remind her of her analyst. This is the first man in her entire life who will engage her fully, take hold on her imagination, make her want to live, if only for him, for those sessions several times a week and sometimes more, when she can tell him about the life she has been living without him, when that life has come to be organized by a persistent preoccupation with him. Of course, none of this can be imagined, not even dimly intuited, by the young woman in heels, who has dressed up in a knit suit for this appointment. She is scared to death, perhaps with good cause. She is going to fall head over heels for the first time in her life with the man who even now is walking down the stairs from his office to the small waiting room to greet her.

She turns around when she hears his footstep, does not remember the meeting with the analyst in London who did not return her smile, steps forward uncertainly, suddenly shoots out her hand. After a momentary hesitation, too small really to be perceptible, he grasps it.

A sequence of provisional selves. Each lived for a season then sloughed off again. This idea latches a peculiar, somewhat demonic proliferation onto our modern conception (which some say began with Freud) of a self divided against itself, deluded as to the nature of itself, when it imagines, as it had through much of the eighteenth century, that rational consciousness is all there is to us.

The seeming stability I imagine for myself as I sit here writing (I am not at my desk right now; I am in an Italian bakery near the Embarcadero, waiting for a psychoanalytic friend with whom I debate the question of authority) may even now be threatened by submergence, as another provisional self emerges to assert its claim to me.

I may be as transient, provisional, as soon-to-be-replaced as was that twenty-six-year-old young woman, who has no idea she has been configured as other selves, or will change so much over the next years. I, who am writing about her, will not be able to think of her as myself, although back then she imagines she is all there is to me.

We are separated by time and development, we meet only in memory, a wispy, lonely ground for self-encounters. The task of getting back to her, to catch her state of mind on the day she begins psychoanalysis, is formidable. If I were able to succeed, that might well imply there is, along with the selves that are constantly created and sloughed off, some thread of continuity that ties together the girl who received the icon, the girl in the turtleneck sweater, the young woman walking up the stairs in front of the analyst with the subsequent selves who will shortly emerge, rapidly, often violently, as a result of her conversations with this man.

It could be I have come up with this notion of continuity in order to soothe my fear that I myself will shortly be done away with. But is continuity really soothing? Do I even want to become the person who might be coming? That might be as unwelcome to me as the idea of collapsing back into the self I was. Suppose all those earlier selves are hanging around, waiting to be reanimated?

Compared to this, fragmentation might be preferable, a discontinuity of selves that closes off awareness of how different we have been, how entirely other and alien to ourselves we might yet become, so that this seemingly stable entity we think of as an "I" would have to be viewed as a mere rhetorical device that stands between us and madness.

But why madness, etc.?

My twenty-six-year-old self also has a headful of whimsy. The large place such thinking occupies for her definitely suggests a continuity between us. We are both brooders. We get onto a thought, we can't let go of it. She has been attempting to make a list of reasons life is worth living. Having assembled the list, she then methodically goes through it, providing arguments against the arguments she has conjured up. This is a tormented game, similar to playing chess against oneself. She is familiar with her entire storehouse of rhetorical gestures, already knows exactly how she is going to undermine the carefully numbered demonstrations of life's value. When she sits down in a chair opposite the analyst, who is a well-dressed man with beautiful shoes, she finds it hard to look at him. She keeps her gaze lowered, folds and unfolds her hands in her lap, suddenly looks him straight in the eye in the conviction that she knows exactly what she wants to tell him. He is wearing dark glasses, she can't see his eyes. This disturbs her, although he has explained to her, when they were shaking hands downstairs, that he has recently had an eye operation. He would not ordinarily be wearing sunglasses.

She says, "I was wondering on my way over here how I should begin."

"What had you decided?"

"I couldn't make up my mind."

There is a silence. It makes her aware how many

kinds of silence there might be, not all of them by any means as disturbing as the detached listening of the London analyst, whom she suddenly remembers for the first time since she forgot her, years ago. She likes this silence. It comes over to her protectively, across the space between them, the kind of silence in which you encounter thoughts that have never occurred to you before. She is very sensitive to impressions of this kind. Trust, relatedness, hope, despair emerge for her out of minute, subtle interactions that most people, even most analysts, might not notice. That aborted analysis of six years ago ended the moment the analyst opened the door to her house. This one has begun well because of this silence, which probably lasts no more than thirty or forty seconds before he says, in a deep, quiet, somewhat husky voice, "And is there something you want to tell me now?"

She starts talking. She tells him about the affair with her therapist in Fairfax, the separation from her husband, her daughter who is three years old, the book she has written, the books she wants to write, her plans to go to Israel to live on a kibbutz, the invitation she has received to take up a publishing job in New York, the musician she has been dating whom she left suddenly one morning while he was still asleep, leaving him a note saying she wouldn't be seeing him any longer, although now that she is back from New York she has been seeing him again, with reservations on both sides, although it was he who had given her the list of the top ten analysts, on which this analyst came in second place. She does not mention the order of the names.

Before the session is over he says words that have never been forgotten: "You are like a bird poised for flight. The next wind that comes along, you will be off on it."

These words strike her. They are the most accurate statement about herself she has ever heard. She is a bird poised for flight. Because of these words, a fierce, muffled sob makes her suddenly desperate to see him again. But he has not yet decided to take her as a patient. He first wants to meet with her three, four times. Maybe he is worried about the affair she had with her therapist in Fairfax? She wants to tell him it was not her fault, she didn't initiate it, she went along with it because going along was part of the bird condition, the being poised for flight. She was then out of her marriage, which was seriously ending; her husband was also having an affair. It wasn't clear who would get custody of the little girl, although certainly the mother wanted custody, although of course she wasn't much of a mother, perhaps mothering is the sort of thing psychoanalysis might teach you?

She is talking too much, he has walked her to the door, she should be heading down the stairs, maybe she shouldn't have said anything after he stood up to say the session was over. Perhaps this talking while you walk to the door is time illegitimately stolen from the time that is after-the-session, so that she is undoubtedly making a bad impression, probably won't be acceptable as a patient, although she would give anything to come back again, for his silence, the beautiful words he speaks, the room in which all this has taken place. It is, according to memory, a grander room than any she has ever encountered in her life before. Books, lightly curtained windows, oriental carpets, leather chairs, a huge desk along one wall with papers on it, as if he had recently himself been writing. She already knows he is the one man in all the world who can understand her. After a lifetime of looking, without even knowing she was looking, she has found him. The first of some six, even seven therapists along the way who has taken hold on her imagination.

And now, what if he doesn't want her?

If this is a self-analysis it will probably have to come up with a case history for itself, some brief notes as to family background, significant events of early childhood, presenting symptoms, provisional diagnosis. This self, born in the Bronx in 1940, father a structural engineer, mother a Communist organizer, one sister, aged eleven.

Father, a quiet, intellectual man, emotionally absent from the family.

Mother, frequently depressed, subject to outbursts of rage, from which older sister seems to have protected younger sister.

Older sister serves as mother substitute when mother returns to full activity as organizer (younger sister aged two).

Death of older sister when younger sister four and a half or five years old. Traumatic.

Family moves to California one year later. Traumatic.

Only surviving daughter sent to boarding school in Los Angeles. Traumatic.

Mother arrested as Communist when only surviving daughter eleven and a half years old. Traumatic.

Father loses job during blacklist of McCarthy period. Traumatic.

Relationship between mother and daughter tense, strained, verbally violent throughout childhood.

Father absent.

Only surviving daughter sexually active from a young age (various accounts of precise age . . . perhaps eleven and a half, perhaps a half year older).

Patient is college graduate, highly intelligent, verbally articulate, intellectual, suffers from obsession with weight and food, a tendency to fragmentation, is suicidal.

If I want to take seriously this casting out of a line to catch the self I was back then, I had better get going. Familiar oppositions have declared themselves: a sense of dread, a marked restlessness, an impulse to get away, to take to my heels. I have come to associate all this commotion with Freud's wonderful phrase "the return of the repressed," an idea that has always appeared to me in the image of a troop of ragged, footworn, weary folk trudging back from exile. The response of the citizens whose lives are about to be disrupted by this unfortunate gang would probably also contain dread, restlessness, a wish to run from the sight, or yet worse, under particularly severe conditions, to take up arms against the invasion. At times, my opposition to this task of recollection has a violent edge. I am secretly scheming to throw bricks at memory.

One of these days this I/she business is going to collapse. Then I will know exactly what it is like to be twenty-six years old, waiting for the one person in all the world who you believe can save you to make up his mind to take you on. A young person may be able to stand that desperate yearning. I refuse to engage this state of mind. To catch hold of that younger self I will instead resort to facts. She, who is always thinking about sex and death, spends most of her vacations in Vienna. She knows the spot where Freud first received his patients in the new building erected on the site of the Ring Theatre, which had burned down in the 1880s. When Freud's eldest child saw the light of day, the father received a letter of congratulations from the Emperor to commend him for the first child born on a site other people had superstitiously avoided. When I was twenty-six years old, waiting for the psychoanalyst to make up his mind, I sometimes woke up at five o'clock in the morning, thinking about Freud's first child, born to a place associated with death by fire.

The person I was back then used to visit birth and death houses, cemeteries and the opera, to which the themes of sex and death had drawn her. At the turn of the century, during Freud's time, she undoubtedly would have been a great hysteric, intended for the opera, before she inexplicably lost her voice. She loves Mahler, especially his songs on the death of children; likes to tell the story how he carried his sister Justine up flights of stairs to their apartment; pretends to believe, when she is at the Vienna opera, that Mahler is still conducting; thinks she probably knew Freud.

She enters psychoanalysis from the literary side, through Nietzsche, Dostoyevski. The analyst she has just met, in the way he walks, erect and stately, in his finely cut clothes, the formal beauty of his language (in which she detects a trace of a European accent), the refined atmosphere of his consultation room, seems able to shoulder this burden of association. Through all the years of therapeutic effort, while she was finding every other therapist a mistake, she must have been (unconsciously) measuring them all against Vienna.

A few days after her first visit to the new analyst she finds out he is a musician, attends a concert of string quartets he has composed, hears people talking about him, is proud to be his patient. (He has not yet decided to take her as a patient.)

In her anguished waiting, reading the signs of his willingness or disinclination (the intonation of his voice when he brings the session to an end, the expressions that don't quite show up on his long, pale face), Vienna flows into her impression of him. Now he contains also her fantasies about the Empress Elizabeth, who was killed by an anarchist in Geneva a couple of years before the troubled, beloved century came to a close. Elizabeth, the second cousin of Ludwig II of Bavaria, one of Wagner's earliest admirers, used to hike for miles and miles on not much more than a liter of milk a day. Her son Rudolf had shot his lover, then himself in Meyerling, a small stone house in a walled garden, which served as the Hapsburg hunting lodge in the Vienna woods. One of these days, if the analyst decides to take her on, she is going to ask him what Freud would have made of this event. Why did the Crown Prince commit suicide? Because he was involved in a Hungarian plot to assassinate his father? Did he hope to dissolve the Dual Monarchy? Were these seemingly political motivations a cover-up for an oedipal drama? Or had he simply staged the eternal confusion of eros with thanatos, that knotting-up of love with death that fascinates her?

These fragments, along with vague, heated impressions of Freud during his lonely years, living in poverty (here she exaggerates), without recognition, getting himself caught up in passionate friendships with other men, forming the Wednesday-night discussion groups, treating patients, forging the first terrible links between neurosis and sexual repression, become almost immediately part of her attachment to her analyst, who must have been, when she first met him, the same age I am now. Unfortunately, this does not help me to know what he made of her.

For her, psychoanalysis has remained a renegade act. If she has sought it out, that must be because there is still alive in it the collapsing Hapsburg monarchy, modernism, fin-de-siècle decadence, the poplars and willows from the banks of the Danube, the restaurant on the Kohlenberg where she once saw a beautiful dark-haired woman, followed her out to her car. In Vienna, our formerly anorexic young woman eats cake, coffee with whipped cream, loses her head over a performance of *Elektra*, reads all of Hofmannsthal's librettos for Strauss in cafés where newspapers are hung from the wall on wooden poles, and where, a mere forty years before, one year before the First World War, Trotsky was playing chess with Adler in the Café Central, Freud was taking coffee and writing *Totem and Taboo* at 18 Bergstrasse, Stalin was in hiding near Schloss Schönbrunn, the Hapsburg summer palace, doing research on the Austrian approach to the national question, while Hitler was living in a shabby barrack established by the city to house men down on their luck.

This city of lies, self-delusions, ceremonial disintegrations, in which simultaneously socialism, Zionism, and psychoanalysis find a home, is the dream world through which our psychoanalytic aspirant expresses her desire to live a life dedicated to culture and art, daring thought, sexual adventure.

That is the reason she has kept her four appointments faithfully with the analyst, although he has not revealed the standard by which he will judge her suitable for analytic treatment. What if he only wants someone very troubled, whom it is worth his while to save? She imagines she could qualify, if she told the whole truth. What then if he found her too troubled to be helped? Send her on to someone else, less splendid, more dreary than he is? Does talking a lot make you a good candidate? But what if talking a lot goes along with talking too fast and talking too fast is a bad analytic trait? He is patient, considerate, clear, precise. When she leaves a session with him, alternately hopeful and desperate about her chances to come back after the four scheduled times, she is left with a vague impression of potential order, as if separating out the chaos of sensations with which she enters the room were a power mysteriously wielded by this man who has mastered the language of naming.

When he tells her during the fourth session he has decided after all to take her as his patient ("I will be able to offer you a regular time if you should still wish to work with me"), she feels something fresh, wild, unchecked, hopeful, violent. These are feelings no man has awakened in her before. In some other discipline, in the courtly tradition of love, these feelings might be regarded as the beginning of love; certainly, they are the beginning of a passionate, enduring attachment, a yearning that has remained severe, implacable, restless, able to reach even me, even after all this time, roaring toward me across the cognitive act of reconstruction that has served its purpose. The hordes have entered the city gates, the dream city is under siege by the repressed returning.

A love obsession, a transference, an initiation process, the student years, the love of the journeyman for the master, the servitude of the courtly lover. Any one of these might serve to describe my first four and a half years of psychoanalysis. Years, it must be said, during which my younger self stretched herself out in the direction of me. When she, back in those heady early days, spoke of self-transformation, she could have had no idea I was what she had in mind. No doubt, if she had known what was coming, she would not have persevered so faithfully toward the goal.

Irony again? We know what that means. In psychoanalytic vernacular it could be called a defense, a gesture of resistance to the yearning that has just charged back to me over the intervening years, sweeping them away to leave me vulnerable to the passions once visited upon that younger person. If I had told my story in the days before Freud, I might have told, about my youth, how it had contained a passionate, disappointed, transformative love for an older man, from which came everything else that came after.

It was Freud's ambition to make psychoanalysis a science, of universal relevance, characterized by theoretical economy, derived from precise clinical observations, supported by bold but persuasive interpretive acts. He was on the side of rationality, against the passions. He imagined psychoanalysis in his early days as a movement of a high, moral kind, making raids against the wayward id, conquering it, replacing its driven impulsiveness with rational choices and decisions. In those days, brooding alone in his study, surrounded by his collection of antiquities, taking meals with his family in silence, he imagined science, reason, knowledge as capable of overcoming the (instinctual, driven) power of sex.

I have never fully believed in the power of reason. I have never been absolutely sure I have wanted reason to dominate impulse. I have always, through all the psychoanalytic years, cherished a doubt about this particular aim of the psychoanalytic enterprise. That younger self, whom I hold militantly at arm's length, while simultaneously spying out ways to get back into her state of mind, would have smiled secretly about these psychoanalytic intentions in favor of reason. She joined up with psychoanalysis on the side of Freud's naming of the unconscious, although she herself had already met up with it through Nietzsche's wild, Dionysian yearning. She knew all about it from the love-in-death drink Isolde had given to Tristan. She did not want psychoanalysis to rush out at the last minute to keep Tristan from drinking at the transformative chalice. She wanted to be swept up in the quest for knowledge as if knowledge were itself a passion. "Everything in excess," she said to her analyst, who said in return, "I would avoid that tendency, Miss Chernin."

It was he who made her aware of these tendencies, encouraging her, gently, persuasively, to balance them with self-reflection, an ability to name, a capacity to tolerate conflict, to acquire, therefore, an ability to choose. Her fascination with him—his thought, his life, his person; his unknown relations to wife, children, friends, colleagues; the books in his study, the pages neatly stacked on his desk—drove the analytic process for her. It was her passion for him that brought her to a first, faint glimmer of desire to plant herself on the side of the rational. If that was the shore on which he stood, she would have to be there too, to stand beside him.

They were, he and she, in that sense, the perfect psychoanalytic couple, he standing for reason and self-knowledge, she seemingly brought around to them, through the power of a passionate attachment to him.

A transference is not always such a passionate business, and this passionate business may have been something more and different than a transference. But transference is the name psychoanalysis would give to the experience, suggesting that the shape and power of my feeling for the analyst was borrowed from an earlier, childhood relationship, perhaps to my father. As transferences go, this one was strong and positive and would have been seen by Freud as a resistance to treatment.

There is a strange, blasphemous daring in this attempt to know one's analyst, even twenty-five years later. From listening to his music, listening to others talk about him, stocking up on the few words he spoke about himself, I have put together the picture of a man who had ended his own analysis because he had decided that it was futile to analyze troubled states of inner life (despairs, depressions, unfulfilled desires, catastrophic yearnings), which would, in the end, have to be accepted as enduring aspects of the human condition. This struck me, particularly when I was younger, as a heroic, melancholy posture. My twenty-six-year-old self loved the romance of it, man in perpetual struggle with the nature of man. No doubt it reminded her of the analytic pessimism of the mature Freud. She probably took to it out of respect for her analyst, in an effort to become whatever this man wanted her to become. If he was soft-spoken, philosophic, given to resigned pronouncements about the nature of life, she too would acquire these capacities. I imagine she never once stopped to consider whether this resignation matched up with the twenty-six-year-old woman, newly filled with conviction about the possibilities of self-knowledge, eager to know more, go further, perhaps just as troubled as she always had been, but acquiring the giddy capacity to give that trouble a name.

If I am trying to trace my descent from her, to enter the state of mind that must have been hers during this early analytic work, I have to think my way back through assumptions I now take entirely for granted, which were, back then, shattering discoveries for her. At moments like this I'd like to give her a good kick back into the past. She seems so naïve, so eager to learn, so trusting, while at the same time prudently keeping her own counsel. I would prefer a more straightforward self as my forebear. Nevertheless my task has been set: I am to find whatever of me was already present in her, impatiently pawing in my direction.

During that first year the analyst teaches her about the hidden link between her wild behavior, and hidden unknown feelings. If she could not sleep at night, if she jumped up and began eating chocolate, if she called a man she had just met to spend hours talking with him on the phone, these behaviors have a meaning. The analyst points out that she might have been lonely, disconsolate, sad about the separation from her husband (a possibility otherwise vehemently denied), scared of caring for a child alone. It seems that behind every behavior there is an emotion, a set of thoughts, unknown fantasies, hidden yearnings. These feelings might have been called up by something that happened earlier in the day, something small, seemingly inconsequential, to which she had had, nevertheless, a strong response. When she tells the analyst about the rude behavior of the man who checked books out of the stacks, he makes a wondrous connection between that encounter and the impulse she felt a few minutes later to buy an entire Black Forest cake in the bakery down on the avenue on the way to her car. It seems that eating four pieces of Black Forest cake could be an act of aggression against the rude man. Perhaps it is also a gesture of protest against the father-analyst who should have been there to protect her. Or she might have been visited, in lost hours after midnight, by memories of childhood, by feelings seeping back over time and distance, so that she, a mother herself now, lying awake in the room next to her small daughter, was herself experiencing, with dread, with outrage, with sorrow too great for a small child, what it had been like to be a little girl in a room where an older sister was dying.

During the first years of psychoanalytic work, by describing subtle inner states, which the analyst names for her, she begins to know the difference between a feeling, hidden during the day, in response to a disturbing contemporary encounter, other desperate feelings that sweep in because of her present rootless life, a sadness and sorrow that belong to the past.

The analyst teaches her how to endure conflict. When she tells him she cannot contain the impulse to call someone long after midnight on the telephone, to run out late at night for a doughnut, he creates the hypothetical situations in which choice would be possible. "Imagine," he says, "that the life of someone you love were to hang in the balance. If you gave way to the impulse, that life would be forfeit. Now inquire of yourself, would you in this dire circumstance be able not to act?"

If it is important enough, if it matters sufficiently, the will to overcome even the most driven impulse will be found. For my younger self this is a startling, dramatic demonstration. Wild as I knew myself to be back then, I immediately grasped that I could overcome the propulsive force of any desire if the stakes were high enough. This seemed a terrible knowledge. It tore away, seemingly forever, the illusion that I was helplessly subject to nameless forces. The analyst had opened a space in which choice was possible. I only had to be willing to suffer enough.

This change marks the great psychoanalytic shift from discharge and enactment to struggle within the self. What I will one day, for good and bad, become has its origins in precisely this analytic moment. Within the self, this is the great, initial turning point, perhaps even a point of no return. It separates me from the girl in the turtleneck sweater, the ascetic girl at the London bus stop, the splinter woman in the knit suit who began analysis. But it yokes me by the most telling thread of continuity to the self who has just begun to learn the bitter lesson of the engagement of will.

Externally, the signs of this great change are domestic, not particularly dramatic. She does not now have to pick up the phone to talk all night to a virtual stranger. She can sit alone at the edge of the bed to observe, and by observing come to endure, the loneliness she is feeling. She can manage not to shout at her daughter when she is irritated, by reminding herself how scared she had been when her mother shouted at her. She can get herself out of bed although she is depressed, can take a job working in a medical laboratory although she is bored to death with it, can stick with it although she has wanted to walk out, and when she does walk out, after several weeks, can understand that she has given way to an impulsiveness that did not reckon with consequences. Faced once again with how the bills were to be paid, daily life to be organized, she can understand the sudden augmentation in anguish, sleepless nights, unrealistic plans to set off with her daughter to the end of the world.

If I ask myself now how these great changes were possible, I would say simply: I had, through falling in love with the analyst, acquired a reason to live. Because he seemed pleased with my accomplishment every time I managed to reflect rather than impulsively act, I gathered up all my resources to inhibit destructive actions. No matter how difficult the struggle, I knew that in a day or two I would be seeing him, would get to narrate the drama of drive and restraint, as I myself, in the small world of my life, began to take on the heroic dimensions of the great psychoanalytic quest to conquer passion. Now I too could respect myself for my growing capacity to overcome drive, impulse, forbidden wish, desire. The analyst's telling vignette, in which will could be summoned to answer the threat to a beloved person, had been analytically transposed. The bond now threatened by self-destructive acts was the taut, all-consuming analytic bond to the therapist.

By the end of the second year I found a regular job in the late afternoons, taking care of the children at my daughter's school, teaching remedial reading to adults at night. I had also begun to write seriously, daily, with discipline. On Saturday nights, instead of hanging about in North Beach cafés, or roaming about near the bay, or driving over to Berkeley to take up a one-night stand with a lover in whom I was no longer interested, I stayed home to read and listen to music, although my daughter was spending the weekend with her father.

In retrospect I can see that a peculiar struggle had now been engaged, pitting the power of analytic naming against the power of emotions called up by the analytic work of memory and introspection. My younger self has begun to look a great deal like me. She can read for hours now without growing restless, she studies and writes poetry, reads the Greek tragedies, reads Nietzsche in German, decides not to go back to graduate school but to make a life for herself as a solitary scholar and writer.

Meanwhile, in spite of this growing capacity for choice and self-control, she is being taken over by an obsession. It seems to grow up alongside this other process of making order out of chaos. It is perhaps a surge of id-driven chaos, wildly, recalcitrantly, asserting itself against the gathering power of reason. That is how she was helped to think of it at the time, although later analyses have had other interpretations.

If I hold this moment steady before my gaze, I see an older man struggling to teach a young woman about freedom of will, the power of choice, the uses of reason, while she, a willing disciple, is meanwhile falling in love with him, whatever other names are used for this state of possession, she is falling hopelessly, one could say desperately, in love.

Psychoanalysis, Freud once said, is a cure through love. It is also a gamble in favor of reason. Because it believes in the vigor of rational thought, it dares to call up the secret powers of the underworld. But what if the gamble does not pay off? What if the forbidden wishes summoned by the analytic process prove more vehement, more robust, than was expected? Who knows what is hidden away on the far side of symptoms and neurosis? Where has it been written that reason will inevitably prevail against unreason?

Thoughts of this kind have begun to occur to our

young woman. Because she is a gambler by nature, she confides them to her analyst. She tells him about falling for him, knowing full well that telling him will make no difference. This knowledge is the love fatalism she has always sensed in herself. She knows the risk involved, surrenders to it, while putting in order the daily world of her life. Every analytic process in which I have been involved casts a similar shadow of unknowing that wraps itself around the proud beam of light that is the analytic investigation. Out there, in this penumbra of meanings too quick, too subtle perhaps for the psychoanalytic net, much of the psychoanalytic process is transacted. Each of my analytic experiences has been set in a fertile darkness, a transformative medium that was never fully named, discussed, or perhaps even noticed, but that has proved more lasting as a contribution to this strange work of self-creating than anything else.

If psychoanalysis is Freud's autobiography, literally in *The Interpretation of Dreams,* elsewhere more discreetly throughout his theoretical work, it is also true that every analysand, as she sets herself down gingerly on the couch, marks the psychoanalytic process with her particular struggle, bending in her own shape Freud's uncanny method of self-transformation. In this sense, psychoanalysis is continually evolving itself through the self-portraits left behind by every analysand on the walls of the primordial analytic cave. My younger self intends to inscribe her name with an exuberant flourish.

She goes around having thoughts possible only to a very young person. She rushes into her sessions to discuss them with the analyst, who never checks her exuberance, the speed of her high-flying associations, the heated spirals in which her thought delivers itself. He has understood the urgency and celebration of this moment. In it, she has been stripped of self-destructive acts by an act of will, temporarily freed from symptoms by a sublimation maintained through the primitive power of love. The lists and counterlists that catalog life's meaning have been shredded. The implacable counting of calories has been subdued. She no longer wakes up at night wondering if she should call that man, whoever he is, however long she has known him, to tell him how desperate she is. She sees no reason she should not carry herself on an equal footing with Freud, who was once (she says) a man who had not yet made his mark on the world, couldn't get his professorship, didn't earn much money, wrote long letters to his friend Fliess, in which peculiar ideas found their first expression. Who at that time could have known (she demands) that Freud was going to make from these odd thoughts earth-shattering discoveries?

She begins to evolve a set of thoughts that are her own. The analyst, who does not share them, debates them with precision and respect. Never once, with not a whisper of intonation, a withheld sigh, a suppressed note of impatience, does he suggest she should be talking about something else. He receives her as one who has come alive through these ideas, is putting them together as the most authentic, passionate self she can possibly fashion.

She is more ordered, more predictable, more reliable. She has undertaken a serious relationship with a man who loves her (not the analyst) whom one day, many years from now, she will marry. She has gotten a divorce. When someone asks her how she has spent her day, she no longer answers with an embellished story. She sticks to her job. She has written a book-length amount of poetry, several short stories, a final version of an autobiographical novel. Her daughter has a reasonably reliable mother, who takes the little girl to the park every day after school, where they do sums in the Japanese tea garden.

Meanwhile, the obsession grows. Now, whenever she is in the park, she imagines he is there too, watching her. When she goes to a concert, she looks for him the moment she enters the hall. He likes Mahler, she never misses a Mahler concert. When she wanders about in the museum on Sundays, to look at the Rodins and attend the organ concerts, she imagines him there, spots him in front of the tapestries, catches a glimpse of him downstairs intently absorbed in the miniatures. In time, every well-dressed man with long hair, deep-set eyes, troubled forehead holds a breathless promise. When she and the daughter go over to the merry-go-round in the children's playground, she imagines he is standing inside the enclosure with the other parents, along with the popcorn and the shrieks of delight and the carnival music, watching her.

Usually, we think of a psychoanalysis as taking place during the fifty minutes of consultation, through a dialogue transacted between two people. This is a pale, tepid conception of a process that has the power, once fully engaged, to transform every aspect of one's waking and sleeping life. I have found the analytic process larger than anything it imagines itself to be, less scientific, more shadowed and mysterious. Psychoanalysis intends to lift the (universal) repression that has come to inhibit sexual desire. A wish, an impulse, a desire has disappeared from conscious knowing (it has been repressed), a symptom comes up to take its place. We reverse this process. We liberate the hidden wish, the symptom vanishes, we are now free to renounce the desire, as an expression of our power to choose, our strength of character, our freedom of will, our ingenuity of sublimation. This is a tidy system and it does not appeal to my younger self. She attributes it to Freud's fear of instinctual life, a residue of his Victorian upbringing.

If repression and inhibition are to be removed over years of strenuous analytic work, the point is, she feels, to give free rein to the liberated desire. Since no one has ever fully liberated desire, how does anyone know what the true nature of desire is? (The analyst listens patiently.) Perhaps it ebbs and flows in surges and tides, tapering off when it has reached a peak, rising again when it has been depleted, so that civilization had better learn to prepare a welcome place for it instead of erecting bulwarks that attempt to restrain it? (He points out that most people would not be able to endure the conflict involved.) She scoffs at the idea of sublimation. The idea that art or culture arises from the frustration of sexual impulsiveness strikes her as somehow odd. To her, now that she has begun to write all the time, it has become self-evident that art is as primitive as sex, or both are equally high-toned cultural expressions. (The analyst knows she has been reading Nietzsche.)

When she looks around for the dynamic that drives the self, she finds it in states of yearning. Yearning is, she believes, far more essential, more irreducible, than sexual desire. Yearning marks the history of every attachment, each retreat from union with another. Yearning is a lament for the lost others, for the bit of self that has been left with them when the rupture of union occurred. While her analyst is teaching her the value of mourning and renunciation, showing her how to name, interpret, relinquish the past, she has begun to celebrate yearning as a refusal to let go of the past until it has been wrung dry of whatever particles of self have been left behind in it.

Sometimes, late at night, she drives out to park in front of his house, staring at the illuminated Indian elephant, while the lights move from room to room as the moon rises. She wonders what it is like to live next door to him, what it might be like to be a member of his family, his wife or son, perhaps his daughter from an earlier marriage, if there was one. Often, after her own daughter is ready for bed, bathed, braided, dressed in her bathrobe and slippers, they go out for a short drive, an ice cream along the way, happen to drive by his house, stop outside with the radio playing.

As the child falls asleep with her head in her mother's lap, the mother comes to imagine the scope of this yearning, which comprehends a larger aim than the sexual desire for a genital partner. The yearning she feels, looking up at his house as it grows dark, little by little losing itself in the darkness, takes, she comes to think, no less an object than the self, but the self conceived not in isolation from the world, but in its transformative engagements with those it has come to love.

With this, she is at the beginning of a thought that ties her directly to me. She is thinking, in a fragmented way, something I, some twenty-five years later, will sit down to work out systematically (and far more modestly), as an approach to the people who have come to speak with me, now that I have a couch of my own to offer them.

I have nothing against those large thoughts of hers, although I know perfectly well only a very young person would dare to disagree so openly with Freud, even at times calling into question some of his most cherished concepts. I admire the stubborn way she sticks to her guns for the entire twenty-five analytic years, through the sequence of provisional selves that are tossed out and abandoned on the way to me. I make no claim to be worthy of such momentous work. I am after all what has come from it, that fact must be accepted.

Because of her yearning for the man who has just now, unexpectedly, emerged from the dark house, has come walking along the small balcony in front of the house, to gaze down momentarily into the street, where she ducks down below her car window, she wants to create a self, a well-wrought, true product, as a gift to him. The desire to become what she might be is thoroughly entangled with the desire to give that self to him, self-love and love for the other knotted in a single, passionate act of surrender to the most one might become, whatever one would go through to create that self.

Some of these ideas are not so distinct from attitudes I have myself since adopted. I too detect in classical psychoanalysis a fearfulness about the unconscious, a not quite trusting it to find its own order and coherence. Even the most radical schools of psychoanalytic thought carry this vague suspicion as to the demonic nature of yearning, rather than cherishing a faint hope as to its potentially redemptive quality. I, over the past twenty-five years, have learned a great deal about passionate states of feeling. I don't see much to fear from them,

beyond, that is, the fear of them, which most psychoanalytic approaches share.

No doubt I have made my younger self less fright-
ened than she was in those days, driving home from the
somber house with the lights of her car dimmed, moving
slowly so as not to wake the sleeping child, who years
later, when she graduates from Harvard and becomes an
artist, inscribes her many paintings with the little Volks-
wagen in which these large thoughts filled with yearning
were first thought by her mother, who, still preoccupied
by the meaning of desire, lifts her up when they get
home, to carry her, without waking her, up to bed.

L et's take stock. So far, I have done what I said I was
going to do. I have written every day at a certain
time, without censoring the emission. This process has
unearthed a sequence of earlier selves, one of which has
rejected the primacy of sexual desire (a heresy for which,
had Freud known about it, she might have been dumped
from the early psychoanalytic movement). She has come
to see yearning as an evolutionary rather than regressive
inclination, sees the love of the self and the love for the
other as indistinguishable gestures, imagines the psychoanalytic transference as one in which the self finds, not
only the history of all its previous entanglements, but the
transformative vessel in which the conflict between self-
development and the sacrifice of the self for love of the
other will finally be overcome.

Well, that is what I have written. But is it true? Did that earlier, upstart version of myself think these things? I seriously doubt whether she had managed to resolve the violent conflict between yearning for the self and need for the other. She was, after all, in spite of many incarnations, not yet thirty years old.

Why then have I written into her history a resolution between self-yearning and yearning for the other which, if possible at all, could only be possible for me, some twenty-five years later? Am I so desperate to forge a link between us? So driven to reestablish our bond I would engage in what is clearly a rewriting of my own history?

Probably.

I think I must forgive myself for trying to make too tidy a package. If I am inclined to relocate myself in that younger woman, that act probably arises from a reasonable wish for self-unification. In that sense, I suppose, memory cannot lie. Since its purpose is probably not to record the truth, one must accept each of its multiple versions. Maybe there is even something touching about this effort to respect that younger person by giving her my thoughts.

Okay, I am trying to get myself hooked up with my earlier selves. Whatever pertains to that theme will show up here, true as far as possible. Everything else, whatever its truth status, will be eliminated. Sounds harsh? But that is, when I come to think about it, what goes on in psychoanalysis too. The infinite material of the unconscious, as it emerges, fitfully, under pressure, in dreams and symptoms and unexpected feeling states, is subjected to a thematic scrutiny, such that your experience, my experience, that of the guy down the block will be organized in thematic categories known as truth. But what is that truth? The five or six autobiographical insights Freud universalized out of his own self-reflection? An oedipal drama, repression, the wish meaning of dreams, a quirky idea about the stages of infantile sexuality, the "discovery" of the unconscious, transference. (Here we go again, a bitter, ironic note. What's eating me now?) I have no argument with Freud's truths when they stick to Freud. As for myself, I have never seen why his truths should be binding for me. I have my own autobiography, far more modest, of course, than the autobiography of a great man. But that leaves me with one outstanding virtue. I am not tempted to universalize mine.

(An analyst would have noticed by now that my claim to be more modest than Freud is itself immodest. I may scrupulously avoid universal truth claims, but here I am holding forth in my own psychoanalytic autobiography.)

Highly polemical, I know. But still, it clears the air, it lets me get going again, just when I had been about to run dry. I have dedicated twenty-five years, an entire adult life, to self-reflection. I have earned the right to my aggression, my violence, my ambivalence. Naturally, I think highly of psychoanalysis. Why else would I have hung around for so long? Does that mean I have to swallow it hook, line, sinker? If I have learned nothing else, I have learned, from psychoanalysis itself, not to idealize. Therefore, a healthy sardonic note from time to time—inevitable, cleansing.

Of course, the question remains. Where exactly do I, in this rise and fall of self-configurations, actually begin? If I believed in a continuity of self, I would probably be able to find crumbs of me scattered along the paths here and there to mark the way to me. If, on the other hand, this daily writing whatever comes to mind is a contrived form of stitching back together the outworn scraps of me, a curious question will arise. Just when, in this psychoanalytic process of seemingly ceaseless becoming, did I begin to begin as "I"?

When did I begin to begin as I? It must have been after my first analysis came to an end. But why did the first analysis come to an end? My younger self had imagined the analytic relationship lasted until one was fully mature. She did not believe in its ending even when she had decided to take off for Israel, because (oddly, unpredictably) the tremendous analytic discourse had been gradually interrupted by an impending collapse.

But what has happened? Are the exuberant early years of work with the first analyst over forever, along with their high flights, tragic recessions? That young woman, her far-flung self flying high with self-discovery, seems once again about to splinter. But what has happened? This analysis had just given the lost girl a hold on herself, the capacity for daily work, a remote glimmer of how to mother. What has shivered this remarkable work that has brought about a self-expansion so fierce I can feel it to this day, in all the pristine wonder of its first emergence?

There have been theories, of course, endless theories. A good portion of the next twenty analytic years will be devoted to interpretations of this troubled analytic ending. Some of these interpretations don't translate well into ordinary speech. *The emergence of analytic material not fully analyzed.* (This interpretation by the second analyst may imply that the first analyst had missed out on something.) *A countertransference not sufficiently understood or managed.* (This interpretation by the third analyst may imply that the first analyst had fallen in love with me.) *A transference not fully understood as a yearning for self-transformation.* (This interpretation, entirely my own, implies that psychoanalysis has not yet allowed for the spiritual momentum of the transference.)

And of course, my own ideas at the time. I have boldly acclaimed these states of panic as marking a profound falling asunder of what is old, outgrown, increasingly irrelevant in myself. Those old selves are perhaps protesting, kicking up an analytic fuss, refusing to decline and crumble. Today, I think these ideas (while true) are also an evasion. What do I think about the ending of that first analysis? That depends on what I allow myself to think, how willing I am to risk loyalty to the past, to that first great analytic attachment. It depends on my mood, the time of day at which these thoughts break out. What do I think right now, without evasion? I think the analyst was not prepared to engage himself with the primitive psychic states that had begun to emerge during the fourth year of our work together. He was perhaps not familiar with them, didn't see the transformative potential in them. I think he was afraid for me, unsure where all this turmoil was going, perhaps (indeed) afraid of the feeling between us, which was perhaps part of the turmoil.

My younger self shows courage. It turns out she has a capacity to endure unbearable states. The old symptoms, with which she began this work, do not return. She does not eat too much or starve herself, she has not reverted to the lists, she keeps her own counsel of desperation, does not once reach out for the telephone. Her trouble now has nothing in common with the yearning for death visited upon the girl in Oxford. The emaciation, the will to starve herself, even the state of being lost forever with which the young nun had gone about her life cannot reach even the outer court of this new terror, the dread of annihilation, the spasms of shaking, the uncontrollable sweat, the sudden, sickening disappearance of familiarity from the familiar face of the world.

There are times when this panic becomes unbearable. This leads to peculiar questions. If you are bearing what is unbearable can it truly be said to be unbearable? Okay, if it is not unbearable (See? Even in this very moment you are living through it . . .), why does it seem that in the next moment you will fragment into disorderly segments if the panic lasts even one moment more?

This assertion, which she made more than once (I can't go on like this. I can't take much more of this. Believe me I am trying, but this is unbearable), has been interpreted by the analyst as a demand for rescue, a pushing of things to their unbearable limit to force the analyst to step in and take control. She does not disagree with this interpretation, but it does nothing for her. During her sleepless nights, she develops the conviction that her body will shortly come apart. Or worse yet, if she manages, through an effort of will, to hold her body together, she might nevertheless fall out of her body. She could also fall off the edge of the world.

She doesn't know (it is a good thing she doesn't know) that these states of disintegration will not manage to get themselves understood for the next twelve or thirteen years. They have marked her with a peculiarly unnameable suffering. This panic will slip through the dense, increasingly intricate analytic explanations. It will still be there, after so much else has been understood.

Much good analytic work will take place but the self's panic will endure, unable to get itself a proper psychoanalytic name, perhaps because psychoanalysis tends to interpret statements about the unendurable as cunning, manipulative, and regressive.

I went into the first analysis with obsessive symptoms, compulsively suicidal thoughts. I got better by shifting the site of the obsession, rearranging the obsessive architecture, so that the obsession could be focused on the first analyst. Then, because I was yearning for him, I could use that desire to maintain an extreme effort of will against the obsessive tendencies that had been my symptoms. Naturally, sooner or later, the whole business would break down, as the will, little by little, gave way before the gathering power of the emotion that had been called up by the analysis, but could not cross into the analytic sessions.

The analysis had cast a shadow that would not have existed without the analysis, but strangely could not be brought into the analytic sessions, although in this shadow analysis I did some of my most profound (self) analytic work. This hidden structure would repeat itself three times, characteristically, in all three analyses: the presence of a disturbing symptom, the emergence during the analysis of a new experience of self, its exclusion from the analysis, its eventual (mysterious) eruption into the analysis, at which point the analysis would dramatically come to an end.

Of course, this pattern can be thought of as my failure to bring into the analytic session what was, during each analysis, of most concern to me, evidence perhaps of a profound distrust, a tendency to remain hidden, to preserve in shadow what the analysis would have dragged into the light. In short, we could regard this pattern as resistance.

Well, why not? That would make it a known, named, by now familiar process, would place it in the category of the expected, the inevitable. For now, it will be convenient to leave it there. My first analysis met with a bad end because my yearning for the analyst (itself a resistance) could not find a way to express itself analytically. This will do as a provisional formulation but we should not be surprised if the idea shows up again to get a good kick in the teeth.

Memory says: A difficult analytic session has just taken place. My younger self has turned to face the first analyst, tears pouring down her face although she would not have said she was crying. So there they are, once again face to face across the analytic barrier. Tears have made her hair wet, probably her hair has begun to curl. If it weren't for memory I would not have recognized her. She is still so pathetically young. Thirty-one years old; no one would take her for more than a waif in her early twenties. But already there is the beginning of something that will later turn into ravage. Hollow cheeks, deep-set shadows beneath the eyes. Another face is creating itself to take the place of the youth face that has just been fatally stricken.

That was the day he told her he did not know what to do to help her. He has said this honestly, bravely. The expression on his face is compassionate, severe. If she has a hunch, he says, some intuition about where she might feel better, he would follow it out, wherever it might lead.

Leave him?

That seemed best. He had taught her what he knew, it did not seem sufficient. They had both worked hard, the work had been deep. She could write to him, stay in touch; if things didn't work out, she could always come back. (She has already been here and there looking for a community where a desperate person might feel at home.) If nothing has worked so far, he says, that doesn't mean there is no solution. She has the kind of courage that will take on any risk, forges on, won't turn back. If he couldn't help her, he could at least remind her of her courage.

She, who thought she was falling off the edge of the world, who was lost on the doorstep of her own home, should take off for a foreign country, where she knew practically no one, did not speak the language, merely because she had a unaccountable yearning for her ancestral homeland, for Israel?

He reminds her how often she has spoken about yearning, which was, she had claimed, the transformative force that must be followed. Whether or not he shared these ideas, they were hers, she had believed in them, why abandon them now?

Has she let him down in some way, failed to be the patient he expected? What does a person do who has grown too desperate for psychoanalysis? Will she be left to fall off the edge of the world?

But these questions are not spoken.

Several months ago, I went back to see the first analyst, to ask him why he had let me take off for Israel, perhaps even encouraged me to go?

I had finished my twenty-five years of analysis by then. I still missed him. No one had ever taken his place. The part of town in which he lived, slow, sunlit streets of stately houses, as I drove through them on my way to him, still seemed a world beyond any world I could inhabit. Analytic time had stopped. In its serene, frozen duration even I was unchanged, although I had grown twenty-five years older.

Perhaps (I had often told myself) he did not want to insult the transformative experience I had claimed to be having by recommending medication, hospitalization? (I think the analyst who later committed suicide, whom I might have been seeing if he had given me the first analytic appointment, probably would have gone for those solutions.)

Somehow, I could not get to the questions. I tried, for the entire fifty minutes, to ask what had gone wrong, why he had let me go, why he had not gone on working with me when I came back. Had he thought I was beyond healing? Had he cared too much for me to be able to help me? I wanted to ask him why he had sent me on to another analyst when I returned from Israel. Between the first analyst and me this question it seemed could not be asked.

We talked about the old days, the person I had been at the time. He remembered the names of my friends, boyfriends. He was interested in my daughter, who had graduated from Harvard. He smiled knowingly when I told him she had become a painter of wild canvases, as if recognizing the mother in the child. But I soon felt how entirely the encounter was in his control, guided by him, shaped, determined. No matter how hard I tried to bring the conversation back to the questions I half knew I wanted to ask, the dialogue unfolded as he intended.

I sat in the analytic room, unchanged these twenty years, the books exactly where I thought I remembered them, on the top shelves the boxed recordings of Mahler's symphonies, one of which he had wondrously given me at the end of a difficult session so many years before. I wondered if he had replaced it. I did not turn my head to find out. We sat face to face, as we had the first time, twenty-five years before. I did not think he looked a day older. He had never seemed young, he did not seem old, although he would be more than eighty.

At first, I was acutely aware that he was looking at a woman with gray hair, who had dressed carefully for the appointment but must inevitably disappoint after the dark-haired tragic girl who had sat with tears down her cheeks, although she would not have said she was crying.

Two

The Second Analysis

(1972–1983)

W as it really I who came back from Israel? I
don't look anything like that hollowed-out
individual. I'm a good twenty years older but
there's more to it than that. I'm not ravaged, I'm not
exhausted, although I have my bad days. I'm not even
particularly ascetic, although I avoid high-fat dishes and
chocolate when I can. Best of all: I'm not desperately
searching for meaning. Searching for meaning? The
search is already a symptom of near-total decline. Meaning is either there in the way you get out of bed, have
breakfast with your lover, take yourself off to work, or it
is not anywhere. Believe me. It has taken me a lifetime to
discover this . . . I almost called it a "truth."

My second analysis, which began in 1972, lasted for
the next eleven years. It had very little in common with
the analytic work I had done before. I was older, had
already made the discovery that symptoms contain
(hide? express? disguise? reveal?) intense states of feel-

ing. In 1972 I entered a classical analysis with a woman who would turn out to be ruthlessly honest and tough. I once caught sight of her, tall, broad-shouldered, in a white flannel skirt on the tennis courts of the Stanford Campus. She had trained in Europe, at the Hampstead Clinic with Anna Freud. Because she was not a formal member of the analytic establishment in San Francisco, she was the person training analysts went to consult when they needed help. She was respected, perhaps feared for her reputation as a straight-talker. She would occasionally answer the telephone during sessions, was abrupt, took care of business, would have been, I imagined, very handsome wearing pants. She seemed out of place in professional suits, occasional dresses. Once, beneath a red jumper, her slip showed. I noticed this as she walked in front of me to her chair. My embarrassment for her brought about the only entirely silent session of my twenty-five analytic years. One day her oldest son got married, or perhaps remarried, both versions told along the grapevine, both denied. When I first went into analysis with her I thought she was probably, secretly, a lover of women, as was I. I imagined she was enjoying a hidden pleasure I was supposed to renounce. She once said cryptically, "You think of psychoanalysis as trying to take from you whatever you love. Perhaps instead it is trying to help you remove the obstacles to it." If this is a character sketch, how much is patchwork, transference, projection? When I first went into analysis with her, although she seemed quite old at the time, she certainly would have been younger than I am now.

Over the years of the second analysis I undid all the modern improvements to our house in the Berkeley Hills. I wanted to restore it to its early condition, creating through it an illusion of a rural house in nineteenth-century Russia, ready to be filled with a large family, cousins, neighbors who came by to stay for a week or two, although in our house there were only three of us, my daughter and I and the man we lived with. The analyst thought my preoccupation with the house might be seen as an effort to restore the maternal body.

A classical analysis means a good deal of silence, a large, hovering attention on the analyst's part, broken by authoritative interpretations of childhood experience, transference, resistance. Classical listening is a high art, austere, disciplined, severe, in which my new analyst would prove to be a master. Never once, during the eleven years we worked together, would there be a single sign of affection or engagement. Yet, I grew attached to her listening presence, its absence of judgment, the analytic precision with which we combed through my life. One day she said that the condition of near-collapse in which I went off to Israel (and in which I returned) could be understood as a failure to have fully analyzed inner conflicts.

Until that moment, I imagined I had failed in my various (ambivalent) efforts to bring about the necessary reconciliation between reason and passion. I must have seen the problem as one of will and geography, how to hold myself together by an act of will, where to plant myself during a process of self-evolution, which was at times indistinguishable from disintegration.

If the self is capable of transformation, that would have to be a bit like kneading a loaf of bread, punching the air out of it, slapping it around on the counter. Fine for the baker. But how does the bread feel about it?

Although I drive down to Palo Alto three times a week for analytic sessions, I often find it is hard to be out of my house for more than an hour or two. Sometimes when I am out of the house I lose all sense of direction. This is one of the reasons I have begun a new analysis. Streets I have known since I was seventeen years old are no longer familiar. I have lost the capacity to locate myself in space. Sometimes I think I am falling. I reach out convulsively but I am on firm ground. These are disturbing symptoms, but of what? Had they been present before, during my childhood? Perhaps they are the traces of a forgotten story from my past. These symptoms might hold fragments of memory, the way dreams do too.

My younger self, intrigued by these analytic suggestions, lets her mind rummage about in its memories. She is hoping to uncover the long-lost experiences behind her sense of ghostly disintegration. Perhaps there will emerge vital, intense, fully present emotions, which nevertheless can be associated with those past events that even now, as she sits across from her analyst, who thinks it unwise for her to stretch out on the couch, might be trying to sneak through into memory, if only through the feelings (transference) she comes to entertain for the woman across from her, whom she cannot love the way she loved the first analyst. This failure is a cause for sober analytic inquiry, which goes on for many years.

If I judge psychoanalysis by what memory has spontaneously stocked up, I would have to admit that, with the possible exception of some ten, twelve interpretations, the other interpretive moments have been swept away. So what is it memory contains? It contains fully sensual memories of driving to the analytic sessions. The time of year, the precise state of the weather, the exact time of day, the amount of traffic, the stream of thoughts already cast in the analytic monologue of memories and associations—that sudden self-reflexive movement of the mind turning inward, taking itself as its own object. This internal gesture brings about a change in the light. There seems to me more of it, saturating things with a pressure of significance. There is a tendency for objects to loom, rush forward, as if insisting on their presence. There are also the waiting rooms, where the excitement starts to heat up, the dread, the exhilaration, the sense of readiness, as of a horse at the starting line, waiting for the gun. Bolting. Starting up the stairs before the light is turned on or off. The shape of the waiting room. The particular chair that is my chair unless someone else happens to be sitting in it. The conversations that never take place between me and the waiting others until one day, during the second year of the second analysis, a conversation starts up. A woman who comes at the same time to see another analyst tells me how her first analyst shot himself while she was in therapy with him. She keeps returning to the neighborhood where their sessions used to take place.

This was the analyst who came first on my original list. This was the man who would have been my analyst if he had given me an appointment a day before rather than a day after the other appointment I was offered, six years ago now.

Would I have loved this man as much as the other, who happened to become my first analyst? Would I have experienced the same feelings, carried over from a mysterious, long-forgotten childhood past, for the man who committed suicide, although he did not read Nietzsche or Rilke or listen to Schönberg. The theory of transference says yes. Would I have come to admire him more than any other man in the world if he had not offered to read my poetry? Her analyst had a traditional analytic approach. She didn't get to bring in her paintings; he interpreted her wish to show them to him as a desire to seduce him. He never knew she was an accomplished painter, she said, inviting me to her opening at a small gallery in North Beach. We did not become friends, although I too confessed to driving past my first analyst's house, going out of my way, driving fast.

Memory has also recorded, from the periods of silent waiting for the session to begin, that particular waiting in which one has no idea what will happen during the session, what ragged thought will suddenly appear, what unknown passage of the self will be negotiated, where the wandering thread of associations will carry one, how one will weep or laugh out loud or grow angry, or want to smash things up, as if one had broken into a hidden storehouse of the self, where a history of one's previous existence has been set down, nothing too small or insignificant for this chronicle, in cursive script, or indecipherable hieroglyphic.

My own exhilaration coming out of the session, just having grasped something. The sudden light in buildings setting into darkness, as if in each window a splinter of hope had been set burning. These comings and goings, along with a giddy sense of being plowed up, turned over inwardly, with these memories is well provided. But only one analysis is the story of a love affair which to this day has not fully ended. Sometimes I find myself thinking about my first analyst, absorbed in the same fantasy I used to have twenty-five years ago. That is how I know there is (after all) an inescapable connection between me and that earlier self, a continuity that cannot be denied, however often I lose track of it. It might be a fantasy of meeting him on Kauai, where he has a summer home, where I too sometimes go for vacations. When I am on the island I always dream about him. And so it happened that a few months ago now, deeply preoccupied by this fantasy of meeting up with him, although I had not then been in analysis with him for some twenty years, I was driving along in my car, I pulled up at a stoplight on Fillmore, looked up into the intersection, and just then he was driving slowly through it, a few inches away from me, with his wife.

I suppose I am a particularly stubborn psychoanalytic case, a woman who won't give up an analytic attachment. But who knows! Maybe the theory of transference, applied intricately during the second analysis, yet again during the third, didn't altogether exhaust the mysteries of love and passion.

Maybe even psychoanalysis can't explain everything.

I've had to do a lot of cutting and pasting recently. Also weeding, clipping back, tearing out by the roots. A tendency to overgrowth had set in, concepts growing up overnight, spreading out, growing wild.

For the sake of the record, I make a quick survey of deletions.

A diatribe about the problems of theory (theory organizes experience prematurely, thus giving it the theory's shape).

A discourse on the problem of origin. ("Original" means no one else in the world has thought this before. "Original" also means: whoever else may have thought it before, this idea has come up raw and urgent out of one's own experience.)

A lamentation about truth (the impossibility of knowing truth; worse yet, the impossibility of knowing when one does know it).

There was even a little sketch of the breakup between Freud and Jung, as it pertained to the problem of wholeness and yearning. Jung, a believer in the possibilities of wholeness. Freud, the pessimist, a believer in renunciations.

Nothing wrong with these excursions. They fit right in with this experiment in spontaneous writing. But they were getting in the way. Now that they've been edited out, I'm face to face with the very problem I hoped to avoid. I've begun to feel what I was feeling twenty years ago. My carefully maintained distinction between now and then has entirely broken down.

No need to make a big fuss about that; it happened without fanfare, practically overnight. All along the risk was lurking in this enterprise. I can't pretend I wasn't aware of it. This does not imply I made up the idea about a sequence of provisional selves. That sequence is the best description I can manage for how I have gone about my life. But one thing is now certain: whoever that was, before Israel, in however many forms and configurations, when that trip was over it was I who came back. I may not think highly of the person I was back then. But I cannot go on referring to her as "she."

In this respect, my writing is behaving exactly like a psychoanalysis. Little by little, the cognitive structures, the outworn metaphors, the organizational themes break down, leaving one prey to the unresolved, the untamed, the not-yet-outgrown, the should-have-been-left-behind. When that happens, you're in for a lot of trouble.

I used to think of memory as a mental event, a record of something. That was before I got involved with psychoanalysis. There one learns. Memory isn't a record. Under the right circumstances, memory rips open into the past. One feels everything one felt back then; there's nothing conjectural about it. One can refer to this as remembering, or the full significance of this event also can be borne in upon one: nothing passes, the past is still happening, time is an illusion. Beneath this civilized exterior we maintain, this maturity, this having grown up to put aside childish things, the primitive child perpetually wails, kicks, falls out of paradise, never recovers.

That is how I felt twenty years ago, when I came back from Israel. That is how I felt this very morning when I woke up. It was still dark, for a good half hour or more I actually thought I was thirty-two years old, had just lost everything. The first analyst, Israel, the kibbutz on which I had been living, the man and woman with whom I had fallen in love, the Arab villages up the road.

In the first analysis, the childhood of my younger self had seemed a fairly wild place, in which there had lived a distracted mother, an absent father, a dying sister. The outcome of this unfortunate circumstance was (it seemed) a failure to adequately develop a superego. The young woman who had gone off to Israel had given herself over to passion. First for a man, then for a woman. No internal rebuke slowed her down. She didn't seem to feel guilt. Moral considerations were not made part of her makeup. She grew up on the wild side, therefore would have to struggle lifelong to conquer the tendency to behave impulsively, regardless of the cultural strictures that kept other people in check.

Now, however, during the second analysis, this view of things has changed. The second analyst is not convinced there would have to be, for this particular patient, a lifelong struggle against impulse. Whereas the first analysis had uncovered feeling hidden away within symptoms, thus clearing the ground for an inner life (self-reflection, choice, hesitation, responsibility, the cultivation of sensation, the fine differentiation of emotions), the second analysis is devoted to finding the childhood origin of impulses, tendencies, character traits. Making this link between childhood and the present is the point of the second analysis. Bringing back to life the self's ghostly remnant will become its goal.

Compared to my first analysis, the second is a bleak affair. Before, before I had gone to Israel, I had rushed to get to my analytic sessions. I used to come early, to sit on the steps outside the analyst's house. The entire neighborhood had been transformed by his presence. I loved the stately houses, the discreet views of the bay, the well-kept lawns, the manicured dogs out on leash with well-dressed matrons. I couldn't wait to tell him about my week, the thoughts I had discovered, the insights I had found, the music I had been listening to, the ducks in the park, the flowers I had gathered from Mount Tamalpais, the richness of life I had discovered.

Now the analytic sessions were a somber affair. I hated the new, dull neighborhood in Palo Alto. I felt uneasy because my analyst was a woman; I thought she wouldn't know as much as the first analyst had known. There was nothing romantic about her, with her heavy, rocking walk, short gray hair, jumpers with blouses that didn't always match. She sat with her legs stretched out in front of her, characteristically expressed herself through ungainly, awkward gestures.

With her, I was no longer engaged in an analytic dialogue, a give-and-take between kindred spirits, a romping, free-flowing discourse on human possibility and limitation, through which in the first analysis I had discovered first the door, then the key, finally the entrance to an inner world, in which a self was being created as a gift for my analyst.

The second analyst said very little. Because she thought I was too disoriented for the couch, I sat across from her, militantly staring at the Persian carpet, because I didn't like to look at her. When I walked up the stairs to her office, I was scared, full of dread, worried about being shut up in a room with her for fifty minutes. It was, I thought, always cold in that room. In the room of the second analysis there were piles of books on the floor, papers strewn over the desk. The neighborhood was prosaic, a shopping mall across the street, there were no views, no bay, no stately houses. I had been cast out of Freud's Vienna, into the next generation of analytic work, perhaps into the world of Anna Freud, with whom my analyst had done her training.

After my sessions with the second analyst, I used to drive back to San Francisco to wander about in the first analyst's neighborhood. Up there, on the hill streets overlooking the bay, I was reminded of the kibbutz in which I had lived during the past year. It too had been high up, surrounded by mountains. There had been no traffic up there, the wind tasted of ripe apples, we had black sheep grazing in the fields. People thrust out of paradise tend to feel desolate, an easy word to pronounce; living it is a different matter.

For me, desolation meant a bleak aridity, a sense that life had withdrawn from me, while I could see that it was still vividly occurring for the people in the first analyst's neighborhood. They were living in the past, a more gracious world, where the problem of meaning had never been sounded.

A ghost must yearn for the world of the living, that is the nature of a ghost. It cannot be done with life, it hangs around, trying to be seen, to taste, to rub up against things. Perhaps it wants to watch over the daughter growing up in the house it haunts. It might even try to make a marriage. That is because of its yearning. A strange, wistful, fugitive recollection of what life had been like. Without this yearning, it would be dead.

During the second or third year of the second analysis, a strange pattern developed. I would be walking in the park, moving along mechanically behind my barrier of immateriality, staring blankly at the static landscape impaled with what I thought of then as sharp thorns of unmeaning, when suddenly I would notice a bird in flight, a child running across the grass in the arboretum, clouds driven by overhead in a frenzy of light and shadow. Then suddenly, fugitively, I was alive, filling out my own body, tasting the air, throbbing. I could weep, I was thawing, I could clap my hands, skip, prance, be swept with joy. I had made it back from my world of the dead.

I would leave the arboretum, the Japanese tea garden, the rose garden down the hill from my house, walk fast to my car, to take this new life home with me to share with my daughter. Then suddenly, always before I reached the car, the gray meaninglessness returned, my ghost world of static, unimpeachable grayness, outside of which, behind me, back in the garden, I could sense the life that was still going on, for the old lady feeding squirrels, the man strung out on hash, the caretaker raking leaves. But not for me. I was expelled, could not regain entrance. I had been violently excluded.

Into this bleakness, as the analytic work went on, there came and went feelings of grief, loss, desperation, mourning. My analyst had the impression I had known these feelings already as a child, when my mother was too busy to spend time with me, when my father was away at work, when my sister was dying. These were signature feelings, the fundamental expression of my self. Beneath all the various self-configurations there had run this continuous thread of unbearable loss, which we now came to think of as an unresolved mourning.

I am sitting with my father in our small kitchen in the Bronx. We are eating cheese. I am a very little girl but I excuse myself politely to go to the bathroom. When I get back the cheese has been eaten. My father tells me I ate the cheese before I went to the bathroom. As for me, I am certain he gobbled up my portion behind my back.

Perhaps this memory speaks, in a coded form, my childhood conviction that my father illegitimately took something precious from me, something that was mine by rights until I turned my back and he consumed it.

My fury at him, the narrow-eyed suspicion I felt, my shriek of protest fill the analytic chamber. My hands curl up into fists. I pound the arms of the chair as if I were beating against my father. I have studied literature, I know how symbols work. It does not seem much of a leap to imagine the stolen cheese an emblem of my mother.

I think well of the analyst for suggesting this, the rage abates, sinks back into the brooding sense of early loss and betrayal.

During the analytic sessions I say whatever comes to mind. That is the fundamental rule in psychoanalysis. Therefore, I try not to censor or weed out anything. This free association has led to a memory of the past, the memory has led to a feeling, the feeling has a meaning, the meaning explains a pattern, from which I might now be freed. In this sense, knowing becomes a form of action. Naming, a way of overcoming.

I feel grateful to the analyst, although I still find it cold in her room. I have the impression, which does not change during the next five or six years, that she does not like me. That's okay with me, I don't like her much either. She is distant, unresponsive, probably disapproving. In time, I come to understand how the cold room, the uninflected mien, the failure to laugh at my fledgling, feeble humor, the unworthiness I came to feel in my chair across the room, have been constructed in the image of my mother.

Sometimes I want to unbutton the analyst's blouse to look at her breasts. I think about this even when I am not in the room with her. This may mean that I want to zip her open, to reveal her, expose her, get power over her, stare at her, turn her into an object, make her come at my beck and call. I did not think these things about the first analyst, perhaps because he was a man. Probably I had these wishes about my mother. More recently, I may have been feeling these things about the woman in Israel with whom I had been in love.

Most of the time I do not think of the analyst as a woman. She does not have the softer traits one often associates with women. Someone I know, who studies with her, has referred to her as an "old witch." When I tell her about this, she does not seem upset. Is she proud to be thought of as tough, unflinching, hard, uncompromising, lethal? One day I discover a desire to run across the room to peep under her skirts.

"Apparently you have some doubt about whether I am a woman? Has this been a question before? Something you wondered about your mother?"

"When I first came to work with you I thought you would not be as intelligent as a man."

"Has your respect for my intellect turned me into a man?"

"I'd die if someone called me an old witch, I would, I'd die, I couldn't stand it."

Over time, I have come to respect the second analyst. I admire the way she pieces things together, makes a wholesome order out of meaningless fragments. Sometimes, very occasionally, when I tear my eyes from the Persian rug, she has a look of wondrous concentration on her face. Then what I am saying matters. She may not like me, but she listens. Because she listens, this strange landscape of self-reflection, this inner world I am cultivating, starts to take on recognizable features. It is not exactly like clearing ground or felling a forest or cutting a path through a primeval waste. It is more like the birth of a world observed from a considerable distance. Mists, fogs, rays of light, recrudescence of shadow, patches of brilliance, the emergence of forms.

I am playing in the Bronx park, in the sandbox. My sister is sitting on the bench. Whenever I look up, she makes a funny face at me. That means she has not forgotten me. I build a round house with a twig smokestack. I demolish the house, build it up again. This time, it has a door made of bark. Suddenly, my fingers dredge up something marvelous. It has been buried away in the sand. I look around at the other children. Nothing miraculous has happened to them. It is I, I alone, who have been gifted with the copper penny. Now I am jumping up, kicking sand, running and shouting.

Maybe that was the day I first realized I was special, not like other children, a little significant world unto myself, with a miraculous, found penny to show to my sister.

Years pass while these patches of memory are returning. During these years I seem, at times, to be suspended under water. I observe great arcs of seasonal transformation, but they do not reach me in my subterranean world. I develop a pain in my knees, I am short of breath when I go out for a jog first thing in the morning. This means I am aging. But I know that in my small world of self I am moving backward in time, getting younger.

A man in the Bronx park has told me I am a cute little girl. I am such a cute little girl he is going to come that very night to steal me away from my parents. My sister is not in the park with me that day. That means she is dead. I run home, I climb the stairs to the fifth floor. I slam the door to our apartment, lock it, open it to lock it again to make sure the man will not get me. But now I am locked in, I can't get out, I throw myself against the locked door, screaming.

The analyst reasons. Perhaps the man in the park is my image of death. Lock him out, you are locked in by the door you shut against him. Leave the door open, he will come to steal you away.

Death has stolen my sister, my father had gobbled up my mother. Therefore, analytically speaking, I find it difficult to form a positive impression of bonds and attachments. Perhaps, in my ghostly state, I have decided to cut myself free from them, or to take revenge.

While I am still little, definitely not more than five years old, I go out alone in the late afternoon and don't come back by the time it is dark. (This memory can be precisely dated. My sister is dead, we have not yet moved out to California.) Down there in the park I hang out with older boys, who play with knives, who light matches. I light a match, burn my finger, come home late, knock at my door. My father comes to the door, visibly worried. Good, let him worry! I shall go on worrying him all my life by running around with boys, coming home late, getting into trouble. Having already eaten up my mother, he now turns out to like her more than he likes me, says goodnight to me quickly when I am in bed, gives me a quick kiss, goes off down the hall, into a closed room with my mother.

Analytically speaking: If I, for the rest of my life, pick up and drop men, get them to fall in love with me, then cast them out, this must be the revenge I am enacting against my father.

If I, for the rest of my life, pine after women who are unattainable, this must mean I am still yearning for my sister. Maybe I am still waiting for her to come home, now that no one has ever told me she is dead.

That means I have never lived a life in the present, my entire life has been a restaging of childhood dramas I have forgotten. I am an individual chained to the past, who has never accepted the death of her sister, the loss of our neighborhood in the Bronx, where we lived next to the park, knew all our neighbors, where my sister, eleven years older, had said one day, when we were crossing the street, "You're with me. You're safe. You don't have to worry."

A few months later my sister died. We came out to California on a train. I speak to my analyst about this trip. Suddenly, I remember how the landscape outside, through which day and night we were passing, is filled with light. There are children in meadows racing along next to the train, there are dogs running about with the children, I see chickens in the farmyards, red barns blazing in a late-afternoon sun, cows with burnished brown spots on them, trees bent in the heaviness of flower, an intense blue stream winding away into the forest, while in our car everything is cold and dead.

My father (the analytic gobbler, the image of death) has been left behind in New York. Maybe he is dead too? My mother sits across from me, staring out the window, seeing nothing. My mother does not look up when the conducter comes by to announce breakfast, lunch, dinner.

It is cold in our compartment. I cannot manage to get warm. I am wearing a sweater, my winter jacket, the conductor has brought me a blanket with the train's initials. When it starts to get dark I sit next to my mother to lean against her. She too is cold, her shoulder burns ice cold against my cheek. When I slip my hand into hers, her hand is unresponsive. Perhaps she too is dying, or is already dead. At night, someone puts the lights on in our compartment. These lights don't fool me. They are a distant glimmer, without hope, lights that have died. Outside, cities of night pass by in garish illumination. We are riding a ghost train through the land of the living. This must be the mourning from which we will never awake, never recover.

*　　*　　*

If I have made and lost many selves, that may have been
an effort to get back to the young self in the fullness of
its self-potential, that copper-penny, sandbox self who
flourished before my sister died. Maybe I too have
needed to live through the death of the self, in memoriam. Or maybe these selves I have lived, the girl in the
turtleneck sweater, the young nun, the splinter woman of
my graduate-student years, the apostle of yearning who
took off for Israel, have each known a necessary life and
death, as each completed a cycle in the self's experiments
with giving shape to its potential?

This is an idea I think up for myself during the fifth
or sixth year of analysis. Because it is my very own idea,
it has the power to bring me back from the ghostly state
in which I have been living. This idea carries an indescribable hope. It means there has been a reason for the
rising and falling of selves, an evolutionary thrust to the
drama of fragmentation.

Then, too, it may mean that the dead selves, those
left behind when outgrown, are scattered about littering
my past, the potential of each provisional self lost to me
until I set out to retrieve it, to rope it back in, to make it
part of myself. Maybe this has been going on since childhood? Perhaps my childhood was already a chronicle of
newly minted, quickly canceled selves, each torn apart
under the stress of its life encounters?

Proudly, during a heated analytic session, I announce

a universal Faustian thrust toward self-completion, repeatedly asserted against the self's repeated disintegration. If the analyst assimilates this idea to her theoretical framework, she does not say so.

As for me, I am busily searching for buried structures, hidden meanings. Psychoanalysis promotes this quest for the hidden truth behind the superficial forms: the "real" meaning of dreams, the "true" significance of symptoms, the repressed wishes that govern the shapes of thought, the "essential" structures that organize mental behavior.

I now associate the necessary next stage of my self-creation with the old story of Isis touring the world to rake up the pieces of Osiris, scattered all over Egypt by his brother Seth, who had hacked him to pieces. For Osiris, god of the Nile, Death by Dismemberment. This myth, told also in variant form about Dionysus, seems more useful to me than the tale of Oedipus. Perhaps I too have been going about my life unconsciously driven by the need to gather up the scattered pieces of myself, torn and dispersed by my childhood history of death and betrayal.

If I go back far enough, if I keep to my task long enough, if I adopt Isis as my model, will I too be able to retrieve all the selves that have been hacked to bits, to gather in their lost potential, to launch once more the cycle of integration and self-renewal?

Because of this idea (in spite of its heretical Jungian

twist), I spend several months in the sunlit world in which my daughter is living. By the time the ghost world settles in again, my daughter and I have been back to the Japanese tea garden, we have been feeding ducks in the arboretum. We have been to the lakes where trees cast long shadows, have hiked out through the golf course along the cliffs above the ocean. During the last years, while I have been growing backward in time, she has become five, six years older. That means she is taller, her hair is darker, she has graduated from grammar school, is studying Latin, plays soccer, knows all the dogs we encounter in our neighborhood. These events, which I too have lived through with her, have now taken on life. The mechanical mother, who has pretended to be living, the robot mother who has tried to go about her motherly tasks, has just been gifted with the capacity to inhabit them.

While everyone else—husband, friends, circle of acquaintances—has believed or pretended to believe this mother has lived through the last five or six years, the daughter knows better. When the mother emerges from her downstairs room (the daughter calls this room "the mole hole"), to greet the daughter when she comes home from school, the daughter knows this is a ghost mother, who has spent the entire day in a world between worlds on the couch in her study, neither awake nor asleep, entertaining what are not yet thoughts, feverishly writing poetry, which is always sent to the first analyst, who always responds.

The daughter knows these things because she has never lost the capacity, common enough among very small children, to read faces. She knows the meaning of answering a question from so far away the question has scarcely reached the person addressed. She has observed the mother involved in dialogue with herself. The mother's lips do not move, she says nothing (this happens when they are driving in the car), but suddenly her hand gestures. This is a silent, exclusionary conversation. The daughter has protected herself from the mother's absence by teaching herself to draw. She can also sew, knit, stitch, embroider, make paper shapes. This child is always busy. Even when she and the mother watch *Star Trek* together in the late afternoons, the hands of the daughter keep going.

It could be said she is making up for the mother's absence by playing mother. She has also learned how to care for the mother, brings her a glass of fresh orange juice when she retires to her study. Keeps an eye on her, doesn't talk too much, calibrates every move to match up with her mother's necessities.

This is not good for the girl, the mother knows it. She would do anything, truly anything, to stay alive in sunlight with her daughter, but after the few months she is back in her gray world, pretending rather than being, for she is elsewhere.

This elsewhere does not show up in the analytic sessions. Nevertheless, this elsewhere would not be possible without the regular meetings, the coming on time, the fifty minutes (never in all those meetings for eleven years one minute longer), the analyst's being there to witness the return of childhood. The ghost self is puzzled, it is reminded of the yearning from long ago that wrapped itself silently around the first analysis, engendered by it, excluded from it. The ghost self thinks about the hours spent in the nameless elsewhere, in a silent watching of the shadow play of unborn self-configurations.

Perhaps the analytic process generates a parallel process, which could not exist without the associative monologue of the analytic encounter, yet strangely cannot enter directly into that encounter. Perhaps the parallel process, the elsewhere, does not fit in with the theoretical orientation of the listener, whose listening (in spite of every good intention), therefore, must inevitably filter out whatever is not compatible with it. Perhaps, too, the self's subterranean transformations do not require interpretation, until they produce the interpretation themselves. Maybe the analytic process does not know how to listen for the birth of the self's voice, which therefore holds itself back, writes its poems, cooks up its visions, mentioned only in passing, then eventually no longer mentioned.

Certainly I try to tell the analyst about this elsewhere of my self-experience, this parallel process that lives itself out in the shadow of the analysis. I believe it is my failing that I cannot invest my self-experience, at its most urgent, withdrawn, secret, watchful edge, with language that is meaningful to the analyst. I can feel her good will, it is a palpable presence in the room, in spite of her silence. Very often now I catch the listening expression on her face, that calm intensity indistinguishable from beauty. In the few and far between of her words, I hear an echo of my own speech. This reassures me. Nevertheless, those silent doings of the self as it drifts in the elsewhere of its self-experience, these urgencies of my inner world, crossing and recrossing the borders of conscious experience, seem to elude my analytic work.

Closed away in myself, while my husband is at work, my daughter at school, I seem to have descended, as if in a diving bell, into uncharted regions. Consciousness comes along, the occupant of the glass bell that holds the necessary oxygen. But there is only so much. That means you never know when the vital air will have expired, when you will have stayed too long, whether you will be able to get back. The tension of this unknowing is with you at every moment, making the descent perilous. It takes a lot of nerve to stay on, attached to the known world by the most slender of cognitive threads. Still, while I manage this, before the panic grows too large, rising into my throat like a fiery ball of terror, I have the impression this experience will never succeed in reaching my analyst because it tends to vanish the moment it brushes up against words.

Perhaps this elsewhere, cast by the analysis, forever

excluded from it, is incompatible with analytic formulation because of the severity of its nonverbal rapture. Perhaps this journey to the far shores of the self can only be indicated by hints, veiled references, metaphors, images of no precisely definable nature, by circumlocutions, evocations, pointings that point at nothing, but direct the gaze to the shadow play of the unknowable, by which my self in its most fundamental gesture wishes to be known. Interpretive analysis is not very tolerant of this ambiguity. How could it be? It was born to translate ambiguity into science.

As a traveler in those misty seas, I have the impression that the world through which I move is far less dangerous than I would have expected (less primitive than Freud imagined the it-world to be). In these self-seas I do not find the clawlike intensities, fanged inclinations, red-toothed predispositions I had been led (by psychoanalytic theory about the unconscious) to expect. If this is an it-world, it seems to be inhabited by my lost selves. These drift by in their tangle of sea growth, most in the grip of another figure, a perhaps-sister, a could-be-mother, a seems-like-father, as if all the lost, old, outgrown, hacked-apart selves, taken down by the history of their attachments, to which they still clung, were inseparably linked to the unknown stories of their decline. On a good day, when the waters are clear, when enough light filters down to us from the overworld, the observer in the bell jar (this self that has left its habitual ground, observes silently) understands the writhing and turning and twisting of these embraced self-fragments. Uncoiling from their watery hieroglyphics, they enact old childhood dramas. There is the time my sister lay in the bed across the room silently, dark circles sprouting beneath her eyes. There is the time my mother stood at the window, her back turned to me, silent. There is the time my father (the mother gobbler) could not eat his dinner. There is the time I met the naked man in the woods, who gave me a dime to touch his penis. There is the time (this self-fragment is kicking) I went down into the cellar with the boys. There is the time my mother and I wandered, hands clasped, through the hurricane. There is the time the building across the street from our bedroom window was torn down.

There are also sea voices, they sing out in isolated phrases, a language of fragments that thrills with a half-grasped import of promises of an understanding yet to come. I listen to these voices, husky, at play on the near edge of audibility (while the oxygen runs out, the panic gathers, the entranced almost-understanding starts to break up, to give way to the now familiar panic of disintegration, as if consciousness knows it has been poaching, will soon fall into a trap, be taken captive, find itself unable to return), as to a language I once knew, have since forgotten.

To tell the analyst about this experience, she would have to be capable of a different kind of listening than psychoanalysis ordinarily provides, something looser, more unstructured, more fascinated by what it does not know, has not yet named, can't yet quite imagine, hasn't conceptualized, perhaps does not believe possible. Listening that is informed by theory, already organized categorically, ready to translate what it hears into what it knows, will probably inadvertently cold-shoulder the sort of experience I was trying to describe, by bringing it too readily into conceptual form.

Not that the analyst wasn't trying. I knew she was meeting me more than halfway, but her listening lacked tenderness, the warmth a shy self needs in the first hours of its self-discovery. Things newly come to light require shadow, they need to be bundled up in their own solitude, with (nevertheless) full assurance about the analyst's presence. For my shy self, the coolness, the distance, the formal neutrality of the classical listener created an uncertain, dangerous environment. Because the self's survival is at stake, the self shows up with a full-blown, uncanny capacity to test the ambient waters—too hot, too cold, too much light in the room, the self shrinks back into its own shadows.

Somehow, my analyst would have to understand that I can drop down into an inaccessible world, come back unscathed, having glimpsed the meaning, the order inherent in the strange dance of it-world fragments. They drift, combine with one another, separate, rearrange themselves, in a solemn, stately dance to a far-off, ever-changing musicality of emotion. During this dance I am fully awake, aware of the squirrel chasing the squirrel across the roof. Yet I am participating in this slow dance of feeling and memory. As I live through these forgotten events of my childhood, I have returned to my childhood. I am there. This may not be possible, but it is happening.

Memory is not only a record, a trace, a scratch on the wall of the primordial cave. Memory has the capacity to take up the past whole, bottle it carefully to keep the air out, then store the past away, outside of time, undigested. When you get used to nibbling at this preserved memory food, you can easily give a slip to the intervening years that have divided you off from what you were as a child. In memory, it is possible to become a child again, breathing winter for the first time, biting the unforgettable first apple.

My analyst will have to understand that I seem addicted to my symptoms, the panics, the ghostly grayness, secretly an explorer of self-worlds that hold me captive. She and I can reason about the reasons I am attached to the past, can't forgive my mother for not giving me a penis, not making me a boy, taking revenge on my father for eating up my mother, for letting my sister die. We can reason about the advantages my ego derives from its symptoms, its unwillingness to leave the past, risk autonomy, step out into life, risk giving up the lost others to which it clings. But we cannot free me from the spell of self-encounter the psychoanalysis has inadvertently fostered, a prodigal child, its lineage clearly established, whose way of life has taken it too far from the psychoanalytic hearth to permit return.

Meanwhile, as the years pass, I get the impression the second analyst is puzzled by me, perhaps in the same way the first analyst was. The second analyst too can't seem to figure out why my panics endure (the fear of leaving the house, the impression the world is about to collapse in upon me, the fear of falling, the fear of falling out of my body, the conviction I might at any moment come apart), while my understanding has encompassed so many truths, the analytic work has been deep and comprehensive, I have shown every good will, said what I could, having finally come to discuss the impossibility of bringing my shadow analysis into our sessions.

There is a recurrent dream. I have had this dream already during the first analysis. It shows up during the second analysis, will appear again, with even greater urgency, during the third. The dream takes different forms but is recognizably the same dream under pressure of theme and variation.

I am on my way to the analytic session. I start out with plenty of time, get on my bike, or into my car, take off. Soon, however, I am no longer on the familiar route, or even in a part of town I recognize. I have lost all sense of direction, everything I see around me is strange. I park my bike or my car, stop in to ask for directions. The man or woman giving directions is helpful, or decidedly not. The panic grows. I am going to be late. I hurry back to my car, or my bike, but I cannot find it. I feel certain I know where I left it. Nevertheless, it is not there. In other dream versions I have completely forgotten where I left the car, start to run desperately up and down streets that grow increasingly foreign as I move through them. The panic grows. What if I miss the session altogether? What if I never get to the analysis again? I give up the search for the car, start looking for a telephone. There is a telephone on the next corner; it is occupied. I enter bars, restaurants, laundromats, looking for telephones. When I find one, the receiver has been ripped off, the telephone book is missing, I cannot get through to information. Sometimes, when I locate the telephone, I do not have a dime. Therefore, I have to start running around asking for help again, trying to get change for a dollar. Meanwhile, the panic is growing. If something doesn't happen soon, I know I am going to collapse. This collapse will take place violently, dramatically. I will fall down in the middle of the street, screaming, kicking. Therefore, I keep going, on to the next telephone, to the next dime. Sometimes, I find a free phone, have the money to make my call, remember the number. But then the call does not go through. More money is needed, or the coin is returned, or the person who answers the phone speaks a foreign language. Sometimes I have a fistful of dimes but my hands shake, the dimes fall, I scramble about trying to retrieve them. By now, I am at my wit's end. I cannot find the analyst, I cannot get through by telephone to call a lover or friend to help me out, I cannot even let the analyst know I will be late for my session. I have ended up in a town so strange people have begun to look at me with an anxious, aggressive curiosity. I have used up my resources, can't ask for help, don't speak the language, am regarded with suspicion, the tension is growing . . .

Always this dream is interrupted by the intensity of my terror, which the dream can no longer contain. It shatters through the dream landscape, the pathetic attempt to provide a holding form for a formless anxiety. I wake up visibly shaking, my hair soaking wet. Sometimes I touch my knees, my elbows, my feet. Has my body held together? The state of collapse, of falling apart, of going to pieces before strangers never takes place. But the dream narrative has been pieced together by an impending disaster; during all the time I am running, looking, searching, asking for help, I know that this disaster is inexorable, inevitable, right around the corner, impossible to evade.

In its basic, repetitive structure, this dream is about resistance. In time, all three analysts will agree about that. Although I make frantic efforts to get to the analytic session, it has been pointed out that I have also dreamed up the obstacles to getting there. The desire to arrive on time, the wish to avoid the session entirely, both appear in the dream, where they are given dramatic, even epic, shape. Analytically speaking, the conflict I feel about analysis, which I do not consciously acknowledge, looks back at me from the dream I have made. Because I dream this dream, on and off, for twenty-five years, taking trains, bikes, cars, stolen vehicles, borrowed motorcycles, buses, trolley cars, the Third Avenue El; because the cities through which I run so desperately constantly change; because the dimes are sometimes tokens or coins of foreign currency, each detail can be subjected to a minute inquiry, revealing a continually changing contemporary preoccupation within the consistent structure of the dream. In this dream, I can also read back the disasters of my life, as if they were yet to occur: my sister's death, my mother's arrest as a Communist when I was eleven years old, my father's losing his job to the blacklist during the McCarthy time. I can analyze all the stratagems I invent to avoid disaster, the cunning I sometimes display (stealing cars, finding dimes in the gutter, jumping onto trains at the last minute as they pull out of the station). I can observe my ego at work to solve the problems with which reality has confronted me. Can't find the way, ask for help; can't find the car, start searching; give up the search, make a telephone call; can't make the call, start looking for a dime; can't reach the friends or lovers, get back on my feet to find that car. Through this dream I can examine my propensity for creating states of helplessness, so that even perfect strangers will have to take care of me. I can investigate my sense of being lost and alien in what should be the familiar world of my life.

In the aborted London analysis coming late happened literally. The dream has seized upon this fact. By now it has devoted years of dream resources to spinning variations on this theme. Therefore, each subsequent analysis had had to decode the dream. In the first analysis, the reason for coming late has been understood as a reluctance to be known by the analyst, apart from the seductive disguise in which I then cloaked myself. Losing my car is equivalent to losing the persona in which I have packaged myself for the world.

This is a good interpretation, one of the dozen or so I have remembered.

In the second analysis, the interpretation of the dream has changed. The second analyst speaks of my attachment to the past, to the sister who died, the mother who loved her more than she loved me, the gobbling father who loved both of them better. Although I am racing feverishly to get to the analytic session, the hidden motive that dreams up obstacle and misadventure must be my unwillingness to leave behind the domestic epics that were my young life.

This too is a good interpretation; I have remembered it.

During the third analysis, the inability to get to the

session on time will have become a fear of bringing myself into the session in a state of collapse. The third analyst will point out that I am willing to talk about this collapse, describe it as something that has almost occurred, yesterday, the day before. But I will never arrive at the analyst's door visibly shaking, my hair soaking wet. Always, before my arrival I will have composed myself to provide a narrative of what I had been feeling just before I came.

The third analyst will suggest that I do not trust him to receive the impending disaster directly. In the last moment, I hide it.

This is a stunning interpretation.

But then again, why should I trust him? He too will have interpreted the dream as a resistance. But maybe my insistent dream is trying to say something about the incompatibility between me and the analytic process; perhaps, no matter how much I rush about to get to my session on time, the obstacle that keeps me from getting there is something about psychoanalysis itself?

Is there a self? If so, what is its nature? Is it continuous, discontinuous, built around a core, or is the sense of core a necessary illusion to keep us going in the face of the self's diverse and multifarious existence, which cannot be said to be singular in its striving toward wholeness and completion? Does the self fragment? Does it have structure? Is this structure a cognitive overlay that disguises inherent disintegration? Is the self an illusion?

These, the most radical questions asked by psycho-analysis today, will probably become the bread and pota-toes of anyone who hangs around with psychoanalysis long enough.

Nothing happens overnight. If you think something happened overnight, that means you have missed the earlier, subtle manifestations. Most things happen by degree. There are minor (almost invisible) appearances of the new; they slowly gather momentum, disappear for a time, return for longer periods, nudge the old self-structures out of the way, endure the backlash of the old dying, suddenly pop up as a new configuration, wide-eyed, exuberant, declaiming all over the place, "Look at me, I am the new, the reborn, the emergent, the freshly created."

That's what happened to me. I was going along in my ghostly condition, with periods of remission. The good spells grew longer, established themselves, endured their interruptions, became the status quo. Was the provi-sional self that now emerged during the second analysis really something to celebrate? At first I thought it was nothing but the return of an earlier configuration. Per-haps the woman who had gone off to Israel had been suddenly resurrected. But then too, the new self had something in common with every self that had come before. It had a pronounced seductiveness in common with that splintering self who had gone into analysis in

1967, although this newly minted self wasn't in love with her analyst.

I think of this self, in fond moments, as the would-be synthesis, patched together around the idea that all the earlier selves, those that had risen and fallen during the years, were now brought back to life, fully integrated, in it.

We may forgive this arrogance, the new self does not have much time in this world. It will last some half-dozen years, then undergo its inevitable disintegration. Out of that disintegration, after another long spell of ana-lytic work (the third analysis), the writer conducting this experiment (the most recent provisional self who bel-ligerently says "I") eventually will take shape.

I don't know if other people experience this rise and decline of self-organizations. Since I have become the lis-tener to people involved in this work, I have met others who change so radically over time one might speak of a self series. But I have not as yet met anyone whose disin-tegrations were quite so dramatic. Why this drama? Why this violence of disintegration? That is the question that will be saved for the third analysis.

For now, knowing nothing of its impending collapse, the self that has emerged from its ghostly condition imagines it will be around forever. In the grip of this con-viction, its illusion of definitive integration, this exuber-ant self goes out hungering into life. It has years of deso-lation to make up for. It starts making changes. Keep an eye on this self. Excluded from the analysis during its preverbal formation, it is the eruptive force that will shortly bring the analysis to an end.

But was it really I (the reflective person sitting here looking back over her life) who suddenly displayed traits of ruthless vitality? I brought a marriage to an end? I went out on book tours, fell in love no fewer than three times? One of these love affairs became (in its own way) a third marriage, which in time ended, to be followed by another love affair, which eventually brought down the exuberant self. This episodic tale belongs to another kind of storytelling. Here it can be alluded to, with discreet distance, sufficient to carry the analytic theme.

What had happened to release the exuberant self? Even for things that evolve slowly, there must be a moment of discharge, when the latent breaks out into the actual. Something in the analysis must have released this self, which had been preparing, waiting, gathering its forces, biding its time, rehearsing its appearance. What single idea could have had that kind of force? What newly discovered piece in the analytic puzzle assembled so painstakingly over so many years? Maybe it was one of those insights that has its own inevitability, that will emerge if two people, in a quiet room, caught up together on a regular basis for fifty minutes, go on talking long enough. In that sense, the idea belongs to both of them. An idea born of dialogue.

However it was, one day when I was on my way to the analytic session, in that dreamy state through which the world retreats as the focus of attention shifts inward, I suddenly decided that all human beings were born with an innate bisexual endowment. An innate, bisexual endowment, yes! The loss of which (I now inwardly proclaimed) was responsible for the self's vulnerability to disintegration.

If only I could trace back the analytic steps through which this thought constructed itself. Undoubtedly there is a complex sequence of associations building up over years of analytic work, sinuously, doggedly, making its way from preverbal rapture into thought. An insight, which must have had antecedents, springs it seems out of nowhere with the force of blinding revelation. The innate, bisexual nature of the self may have been an idea I first tried to think up when I lived in Israel, where I found myself in love with a man and a woman in my kibbutz. Perhaps the idea had been driven out by other urgencies or was saved up for a last-ditch effort to cast a theoretical net around my disintegrations. Perhaps I needed to make my way back through an overgrown childhood experience before I could grasp the relevance of this idea. The pathway is lost. The idea still holds its original fascinations.

I reasoned: under severe social coercion, this natural, bipolar sexual existence of the young child must have been forcibly broken up as the child was compelled to choose exclusively the male or female orientation. From the moment the choice was fatefully made in the life of the child, one-half of the self's potential had been exiled, driven out of existence, shut away in a solitary confinement, where it pined for its reemergence, growing desperate, violent, frustrated, hostile, launching subterranean attacks on the survivor half-self (symptoms, slips, jokes, phobias), all because it was not welcomed back into the life of the self, to complete it, to provide it with the missing half of its requisite wholeness.

Mind observing itself is mind changing itself. By the time mind theory has dried its wings, mind has moved on, the theory is done for. Even suppose Freud had managed to describe accurately the state of mind of patriarchal, Victorian Europe. Even before his ink had dried, the mind he had observed, precisely because he had just named it, would have been launched on its insidious work of self-transformation. What do the soul, the psyche, the self have in common? Their infinite capacity, their impenetrable darkness.

Of course, back then, I had no idea that I, with this bisexual thought, was rehearsing a psychoanalytic priority drama from the early years of the century, when Fliess first told Freud about innate bisexuality, then became alarmed that Freud would publish the idea as his own. Freud, acknowledging his friend's claim, held off the publication of his work for several years; then finally, apart from a passing reference to bisexuality in *Three Essays on Sexuality,* he dropped it as the central explanatory principle for repression. Nevertheless, Freud leaked the idea to one of his patients (Swoboda, later involved in a plagiarism suit), who mentioned it to a friend (Weininger, who later killed himself). Both Swoboda and Weininger brought the idea of bisexuality to public attention, thereby depriving Fliess of his rightful claim to it, a circumstance that caused the final breach in the strained relations between Freud and his former mentor.

An idea that doesn't get placed, gets driven into a corner, gets quarreled over, causes a breach, makes enemies, starts scandal will return, if only almost a century later to an exuberant hothead, who is racing up the stairs to the analyst's office, running down the hall into the waiting room, where she is of course too early (she has to keep the dream from coming true). She goes outside again, strolls fast up and down the block, goes over to the shopping mall across the street, wanders about in the halls, checks the time constantly, races up the stairs, down the hall, into the waiting room, where the signaling light has just been turned on. The excited one, the analytic patient who used to be a ghost, goes racing up the stairs, heart pounding, practically knocks the analyst over (this is an exaggeration) in her eagerness to get into the analytic chair to tell the analyst what has just occurred to her.

The analyst does not seem surprised. She too has read Freud. She knows the exact passage in the *Three Essays* where bisexuality is mentioned. Of course the essays might have profited from the bisexual explanation. This idea is not new to her. Nevertheless, she receives my excitement with the large, serious listening that makes her suddenly beautiful. Her face, perhaps against its own inclination, registers interest, respect for me, a tender appreciation for her analysand's self-discovery of those great analytic thoughts with which the second analyst must be thoroughly familiar. The idea of a suppressed bisexual tendency might have led Freud away from drives to cultural prejudice and coercion. The bisexual idea might have shifted Freud's gaze from internal forces to the enormous cultural pressure exerted against small children, causing splitting, self-division, a catastrophic loss of wholeness, a one-sided, conflictual development with a good half of the self sliced out of the picture. If Freud had gone on to develop the idea of bisexuality, he might have anticipated the androgynous, revolutionary cast of late-twentieth-century feminist thought. He could then have derived symptoms, neurosis, civilized discontents, from the dynamic conflict between the severed halves of the gendered self. He could even have explained Kim Chernin.

As for myself, even if I can no longer take myself quite so seriously, I am shaken, here at my desk, by the charge of sheer intellectual excitement that filled the analytic session fifteen years ago. I can feel the shattering force of this seeming revelation: all human beings are bisexual according to Freud, according to nature.

And therefore, so am I!

Freud and Fliess may have speculated about these arcane matters during meetings together at Achensee but (so far as we know) they did not live out the theory. For most people the discovery of innate bisexuality remains a symbolic event, a question of gathering back alienated potential. For men, the ability to be swept by primal tears. For women, the freedom to charge out, strutting, triumphant.

For my newly configured synthesis self, theory only has meaning when put to practice. If a good half of me has been locked away, under pain of social censure, time has come to welcome it back from its exile, liberate it from the constraints of theory, let it roar.

With this thought, with its exuberant declamation, its immediate relevance, its capacity to explain my history of yearning and disintegration (during which I must have been organizing and disorganizing self-configurations around forbidden patterns of desire), a self is launched that deserves to have its day. I begrudge it nothing.

In my analytic work I now begin to trace my bisexual lineage. Apparently, bisexuality is still there by the age of six, when a little girl comes home from school with me, runs excitedly into the back bedroom, shows me her tush. With equal enthusiasm, I lift my dress, pull down my pants, show her mine. We are looking very seriously at one another over our shoulders. Then, backing toward one another, with all the subtlety and precision of accomplished lovers, we gingerly touch, flesh to flesh in our nakedness. In that moment, I feel exuberantly certain that I am a little boy.

The tendency to configure myself as a little boy in love with little girls undergoes a period of quiet during my exuberant attachment to the boys in my fourth-grade class. This involves square dancing, exchanging valentines, a date with Minkoff to the newly released horror movie *The Thing*. He arrives in a suit, he pays our way on the bus, he buys the popcorn, we hold hands in the third row of the movie in downtown Los Angeles. After that, although we are only ten years old, I am his girlfriend. Dancing the square with other boys as my partner (which I do) playing with other boys after school (I am incorrigible) is considered a betrayal. The pattern of my attachment to men has clicked into place. In the coatroom, while the teacher is busy teaching reading to the slower kids, Richard Daly, Donald Greenberg, Jerome Katz, and I write a book about sex. It also has drawings of male and female parts. We develop a theory: when babies are desired, the mother and father go to the hospital, where the doctor shows the father how to stick "it" into the mother. Where remains somewhat ambiguous.

Because the neighborhood is changing, because it is no longer exclusively white, Ronnie Minkoff and his family move away. Thereby sparing their son, I say to my analyst, who does not smile, what would no doubt have been a highly traumatic childhood entanglement with a prepubescent femme fatale.

A few years later, in junior high school, sex means heavy petting, boys coming over after school while my parents are at work, dancing up close with all body parts touching, it includes orgasms and outrageously exploratory oral undertakings. This is, I inform the analyst, the routine heterosexual course of the young girl of the twentieth century, half of whose sexual potential (passive, female) has evaded repression, at the expense of the other half (desiring, male) which therefore pops up intermittently.

At the age of thirteen, I suddenly take to spending my weekends courting a young black girl who lives a few blocks away from us, near our high school. I get dressed up in my ten percent cashmere sweater, a newly ironed pair of jeans, my white bucks. I go to call on her. This takes place on Saturdays and Sundays. Her mother comes to the door, looks out through the small grate, says, somewhat impatiently, "Beverly, that little white girl's here again."

Beverly appears, grabs my hand, pulls me down the stairs into the street, where we race all the way to the drugstore for lime-green sodas. They are my treat. I am the admirer, the courtly suitor. This means I who put my arm around her shoulders, worship otherwise from a respectful distance.

At school, although we have several classes together,

I maintain this distance. I enjoy my secret love, the virility it bestows upon me. We eat lunch in the same part of the schoolyard, among the same group of friends, but not together. I wave to her in the hall, then pass by quickly. Sometimes I hang around her locker. I have always been interested in boys; now I am interested in a girl too. Saturdays arrive, the jeans get ironed, the white bucks get beaten with the chalk bag, I am on the way, hands in my pockets, whistling, to see my girl.

The analyst wonders how this courtship came to an end.

Memory is speechless.

In time, it produces an event out of its store of the willfully forgotten. There is a night in late spring. Beverly and I are wandering around our neighborhood. In those days parties were loud, everyone was invited, you heard the music, headed out in its direction until you saw kids sprawled out on the lawn drinking from bottles wrapped in brown paper wrappers. That night, a boy with straightened hair danced three times with Beverly, who seemed to have forgotten about me. That was the night I discovered (without naming it; the naming came later during psychoanalysis) the disadvantage of growing up in a society that allowed only one pole of the bipolar sexual orientation. Because I was a girl, was dancing with a boy, was wearing a tight skirt, large earrings, high heels, I could not ask my love to dance with me.

That same night, slightly drunk, she in the front seat

with her guy, I in the back seat with his best friend, way past midnight when we should have been home in bed, Beverly and I gave ourselves to each other through those forgotten boys. I managed to look over into the front seat, where Beverly was lying with her knees raised, her skirt up around her waist, her eyes closed tight, while the boy with straightened hair turned to look at me. That wink (its infinitely untouchable superiority) was not needed. I had already tasted the full exclusionary meaning, the privilege of being male.

From that night until the age of seventeen I enjoyed boys for the way they had remained ignorant of the female potential they had sacrificed in themselves for the achievement of their virile, breathtaking masculinity. (The analyst thought I had identified myself with the attraction the boys felt for me, thereby resolving for the time being the tensions of my conflictual yearnings.)

At the age of seventeen there is another passion for a woman. She has my sister's name, the same brown eyes. We are traveling together in China, I am the youngest person on the trip, we share a bedroom, my love is chaste, discreet, infinitely modest, a secret yearning that never dares to name itself desire. Probably this is because of Fliessian repression.

But now in the second analysis this archaic yearning has emerged. It has given itself a name, shaped itself as desire. Therefore, I can explain the ghostly self, which must have retired from life out of sheer inability to resolve its conflict, welcome back its secret-sharer, come to terms with its double nature.

The analyst listens quietly.

Nevertheless, I have just begun to imagine that psychoanalysis is not (necessarily) trying to free me from inherent bisexual tendencies by establishing a more efficient form of repression. On the contrary, I am now free to choose (if that is my choice) a bisexual wholeness.

The analyst points out: not everyone has to translate theory into practice. Freud and Fliess, for example, regarded adolescence as a time when the repression of the missing half-self would be vigorously renewed. One could certainly not regard them as champions of sexual freedom. Freud believed in somber renunciations. I too, if I wish to follow in Freud's footsteps, can celebrate my inborn duality, find a sublimated, symbolic form for its expression, and leave it at that. Perhaps (as Freud once did) I will travel to Rome, submit myself to the power of Michelangelo's naked, nubile, seductive David.

Raw power of feeling, the naked edge of any event, pushing things to the limit, testing theory against lived experience, that's for me. Later on, when I too become a listener to other people's evolutionary work, I will discover how many possible half-selves and core-selves can be named, discovered, imagined, configured. Back then, being relatively young, I believe my self theory has a culture-shaking, universal relevance. I can now make sense of our human tendency for perpetual conflict, the rise

and fall of universal inhibitions, the recurrent anxieties
that plague our kind. As for me, I can state my case with
a definitive formulation: all along through the rise and
fall of selves, there have been two self-organizations, one
of which (female) had been permitted to thrive, while
the other (male), had been brutally banished, taking
away with it virilities, proud self-assertions, the sheer,
unashamed boldness of its desires.

This newly configured self. No reason really to mention its flaws. Its vulnerability to anxious states; a
tendency to fly off the handle when not understood; a
habit of making and dropping friendships, lovers; a preference to work in spurtlike inspirations, then fall tired,
then fall silent, then fall into despair. Surely, given its
moodiness, its ambiguities, it is not what anyone else
would call a stable self. Perhaps it is fortunate that, during the years of its reign, the daughter grows up, goes off
to Harvard. This is fortunate for the daughter, but it
removes one of the restraining elements that have kept
the mother in check.

The analyst does not seem unduly disturbed by this
self's flights and fancies. Occasionally, she can be caught
smiling, once she laughs, then immediately recovers herself. When the exuberant self comes back shaken from
its experiments in bipolarity, the analyst helps it to tease
apart its newly emerging conflict. It is one thing to proclaim the dual nature of the self, another to seek its inte-

gration. That takes an epic battle between two equally powerful opposing forces, the repression that preserves the half-self, the yearning that seeks the self's reintegration. Of course, the reigning half-self will lash back against its would-be usurper.

The analyst is persevering. She seems, within her benign neutrality, pleased when I begin to publish books. In this way, little by little, she helps the exuberant self into the world, analyzing its fear of speaking in public (everything it has kept hidden will suddenly be revealed); its terror of envy (if anyone knows I have this gift, this amazing orgasmic wholeness, they will try to steal it from me); its tendency to hide its light therefore under a bushel, its strategies of concealment, among which suffering has been given a leading role.

Every analytic session holds new insights, new discoveries; the time flies by, there is never enough time to tell it all, especially now that there are so many adventures and the sessions have dropped to twice, then once a week, as the bi-self flourishes in newfound independence. Even the terrible, six-week vacations, which tormented the ghost self, now go by in a dignified fashion. The exuberant whole-self has no need to drive all the way down to Palo Alto to drive past the analyst's office, knowing full well she is not there. She has been, for the ghostly person who could not attach herself to the present, the root, the anchor, the mooring, without which there had not been movement

through time, simply unbearable waiting for the analyst's return.

And so it happens that during this time the third
marriage also ends. I fall in love with a woman who lives
in New England. Although I have never met this woman,
I have written letters to her, we have spoken once on the
telephone. At the end of the first conversation I have,
inexplicably, told her that I loved her.

During the next analytic session, I storm against
myself. The analyst agrees, I am living in fantasy. She
points out that I have always been a believer in fantasy.
What objection do I have to living the fantasy out?

How's that? I am going to run off for a four-day meeting in Boston with a perfect stranger? No analytic objection to that? A stranger with whom I am in love? Whom
I have never seen? Whose voice I have heard once on the
telephone?

No analytic objection?

I, who can now use analytic tools proficiently, have
already figured out that this woman from the East Coast
is my sister, whom I left behind more than thirty years
ago, when no one told me she had died.

The analyst listens.

Therefore, I point out: I am an anxious person. I am a
hothead, I have periods of elation and despondency, I
can't be relied upon, I make promises I can't fulfill, get
swept away by enthusiasms, draw people into an orbit of
excitement, disappear, can't be held accountable.

Surely this is not a person ready to stop analysis?

Once before, some twelve years ago, I had left for Israel in a state of nervous excitement, seeking a refuge. Now I pack my books, rent my house, say good-bye to my friends, move back to Massachusetts, to take up a relationship with a woman I have known (by that time) for four days. On the basis of that passion, the fantasy I have spun around her, the yearning that draws me to her, I am giving up my home and friendships.

Analytic silence.

Perhaps, in spite of my various anxious states and their defenders (minor claustrophobia, occasional agoraphobia, small phobias, a few remaining compulsions), the second analyst trusts sufficiently in the integrity of the self I have evolved? There is something to be said for that. From the moment the exuberant, would-be whole-self emerged, there would never again be a wholesale shattering. This self, although it is fated to undergo further disintegrations, has a firm hold on the world. Therefore, it is different from any self-configuration that has emerged before. From now on, no matter how stormed by conflict, it will write books, earn a living, make a name for itself, even in time become an analytic listener, practicing a different kind of listening to the unheard selves of others.

Perhaps this is why the analyst feels the analysis has come to an end. Perhaps this is an act of extraordinary courage on her part. Letting me go, without caution, without warning, into a life that promises to be as wild, as impulsive as suits my nature? This must be the awesome accomplishment of the almost impossible analytic neutrality Anna Freud defined: that equal distance from the expressions of id, ego, superego. The analyst might not run off to New England because she has made love to a woman for four days, Freud and Fliess might not have decided to live out their bisexual theories, but why should my life fail to take its own course?

I feel an enormous respect for psychoanalysis because it has shown this courage, this willingness to trust the spontaneity of the self, thrusting itself forward, regardless of dangers. There is, in my eyes, something even heroic about the second analyst. For these qualities, for the first time in the eleven years I have known her, I fall in love with her.

I had tried to end the second analysis several times before I moved back to New England. Several times I had failed. The first time, archaic symptoms, sloughed off with an earlier self, rose up vigorously to protest the analytic absence. The various fallings through space, out of the body, off the end of the world, forever. The incorrigible sleepless nights made worse now by the terrible question. Had I spent those fifteen analytic years for nothing?

Was there something unfixable about me? Was I wounded beyond repair? Was I wedded to my own destruction? These, the unsleeping interrogations, drove

111

me back into the second analysis, where they were shown to be secret pessimisms about the self, bleak forecasts of its inevitable sufferings, which the analysis had not yet uncovered.

Another ending was shattered by a return of the panic states that had driven me to Israel. After the third ending the analyst went on vacation. I did not plan to see her on her return, I was moving to New England. But I was waiting for her when she came back, my departure briefly postponed.

Some people think of the self as an onion. The self-onion is then analytically peeled. Some people think of the self as a circular staircase. You complete the first circle, the spiral begins again at a lower level, the same pattern of stairs, the same thematic structure, only this time you have descended further into the self's recess. It is understood: there is no bottom to the self's depth. Some people choose to go on down into the next circle but analysis can legitimately end each time a spiral has been chalked off. In that sense, unless you are stalking the infinite, there will always be something arbitrary, chosen, fallible about an analytic end.

That is how I reasoned on the plane to Massachusetts, during the trip up the coast of Maine, when I was settling myself in a rented house in the country. But when my troubles start again, less than a year later, when I move back abruptly to the West Coast, carry on a turbulent relationship, with telephone calls and flights back and forth across the continent, anxiety reaching a new pitch, the theme of disintegration sounding again, distantly, then growing closer, I begin to have an uneasy thought.

What if the second analyst had let me go because, like the first, she no longer knew how to help me? The second analysis had ended, as had the first, with an eruption of feeling, followed by a departure. Both times the departure had been followed by a love affair that took place far away. At the end of the recent love affair I return to the Bay area, as I had returned from Israel, to find that the analyst wants to refer me to someone else.

The reason for this referral will occupy a significant place in the third analysis. What if the second analyst was, for all her apparent patience, also at her wit's end, not knowing what to do with me, having nothing more to teach me? What if my experience had once again proved incompatible with psychoanalysis? What if the mysterious elsewhere, cast by analysis, exiled from it, erupting into it through passionate states, would always prematurely bring my analytic work to an end?

What if the analyst had "encouraged" me to move to New England because she was tired of working with me? What if she had used up her store of interpretations for why I had trouble with endings, separations? What if she couldn't figure out any other way to bring the analysis to an end? What if she simply didn't want to have anything to do with me when I came back?

It occurred to me recently, at the end of a day's writing, that the second analyst, as perhaps also the first, had offered me as fully as possible her subjective, personal knowledge of psychoanalysis. She would have known there were shadows, hidden depths, obscure byways no single analyst can explore.

Back then, I thought she had concluded I had better just make peace with my life. I wrote books, I worked as a writing consultant, I consulted with women about their troubles with food. Perhaps, as the first analyst, all those years ago, she too thought I simply had to accept my life for what it was? But it was, once again, I thought, threatening to disintegrate. I did not know that its disorders would now be held by a self-structure that would endure all future threats to its integration.

All future threats?

Well, so far.

Three

The Third Analysis

(1984–1992)

It is two o'clock in the morning. There has been a bird singing at night, an accomplished coloratura. I do not know the name of this bird but I am grateful to it. Because it intermittently sings, I believe in the passage of time. I know, sooner or later, it will be morning. At any moment the phone might ring. That would be the woman from New England. That would mean the quarrel starting again, the reasons I moved back to New England in the first place, the reasons I left.

All disintegrations have a lot in common. This can give you the impression you have not made progress. Now you are forty-four years old, but you feel exactly the way you used to when you lay in bed at seventeen wondering how to survive through the night. Is this true? No it is not. There is something new about this disintegration. The self-configuration I have lived during the last five years is about to fall—yes, I know this. A new self will be established to take its place. I may not wish to admit this knowledge, I may prefer the more dramatic, tragic version, but I cannot entirely evade the truth: I am a self who will probably hold together through all my downfalls.

Nevertheless, disintegration is not a pleasant feeling. It can also not be described. There is no reason to believe that if something doesn't happen to intervene you will simply not hang together. What could this mean? If you came apart, what would happen to the parts? Would they float off into space, lacking the specific gravity of their integrity? Would they yearn for one another? Would they race blindly about, like a chicken with its head cut off? Would the body's intelligence have survived in each part, so that each part might then hastily seek a strategy for reintegration?

Perhaps, if the disintegration takes place suddenly, in spite of all one's efforts to keep it back, all parties to the dismemberment will instantly forget their prior allegiance, their kinship, their having been the left and right of an ordained bodily symmetry. Where then would the self be? Fragmented into each fragment? Hovering above the mess? Desperately trying to locate itself in something?

How much time would it have before it too was obliterated?

What if it cried out? Would a cry without a body be heard?

These thoughts are unpleasant. Anyone to whom they are occurring will get the impression they better do something, time is running out, things are getting desperate.

The problem is. To whom will you turn? You may have already checked in with the second analyst, who does not presently have time in her schedule. She may have given you the name of another analyst. You may not want him, because he is a man. You think a man may not know as much as a woman. Would this man understand the innate bisexual nature of the self?

It is three, then four o'clock in the morning. The bird has not sung for a good hour or more. This means the bird may never sing again, time will have stopped passing. If time has stopped passing, that means the body will not be able to come apart. That is good. Unfortunately, it also means this moment will never change, the disintegration will always be about to happen, no one will be able to apprehend the cry, to come to help you.

A good analogy for the terror: the man lying beneath the pendulum as it swings closer, closer.

Five o'clock. I pick up the telephone. I dial the number of the psychoanalyst to whom I have been referred, a neighbor apparently of the second analyst, his office across the street from hers, his name familiar to me from his writing. His voice on the telephone machine is calm, steady, intelligent, quiet. I instantly like this voice. I believe in its capacity to hold me together.

I leave my name, telephone number, the name of the second analyst. I do not say I am about to shred into tiny

119

pieces that may never be able to be put back together again. I do not say this is an old symptom, which has been analyzed before.

The bird sends out its silver cascade, the entire song, usually delivered in broken phrases. I hear in this nocturnal song a far-flung reminder of the self's integration. This fugitive feeling (let it be called hope) may have something to do with the new analyst. I have read an article he has recently published. In it I have discovered a mind of unusual precision and clarity. It is the sort of mind to which I could tell my own story. It is also a mind with an unusual gentleness, it has softness, in spite of its brilliance, a kind of almost offhand tenderness toward the small children he describes, whose awareness of being a self he has begun to document.

Because I believe in this man's capacity to help me, even before I have met him, I have begun the analysis with him in a state of highly positive transference.

The phone rings. Must be the woman from New England. I let it ring twice, pick it up fast on the third ring. Although it is still only six-thirty in the morning, the new analyst has received my message, returned my call.

For that, for knowing how much I have needed to hear from him, for calling while it is still not quite light, for speaking in that calm voice which offers an immediate appointment, I am what will prove to be, in spite of forthcoming disagreements and an eventual divorce, to this day, deeply grateful.

In gratitude then, at six-thirty in the morning of an early summer day, my third analysis has just begun.

I look up fast when he comes into the waiting room. I believe in first impressions. He is an exceptionally slender man, not much broader than I am, he is wearing a suit and tie, is bald, seems shy, his eyes take me in kindly, with penetration, an awesome penetration. I too am reading him. Perhaps I am the same kind of reader. One glance, I know with whom I am dealing. Unless all this is a fantasy, a projection, one more of my eternal self-delusions. Then, he smiles.

Has an analyst ever smiled before at first meeting? This smile seems out of place, incongruous, not an expected part of the analytic process, therefore I find it deeply reassuring. It gives me the oddest impression that this man is prepared to care about me. That he will understand me I have no doubt. This I have determined from his articles. I have, as yet, after all these years, much faith in the analytic process. I trust him to be a hard-working, perceptive analyst. If analysis has not yet helped me overcome my extravagant disintegrations, that doesn't mean it cannot help me. A man like this, who might be even younger than I am, who is gentle, who has a mind sharp as a diamond, has just smiled.

All this has transpired during the initial two or three seconds before he walks across the small room to turn out the light on the signal board. Already it means a great deal that he comes into the waiting room to fetch me. Our communication is not to be through an impersonal code of lights. I have signaled him, he has come to get me.

This is the second time.

Seated across from him on the top floor of a modern building in a shopping mall, I observe dark circles beneath his eyes. That means he too has suffered, has a profound, perhaps even turbulent inner life, he has lived through a lot, perhaps even today is going through something, which he has overcome on my behalf, to listen to me.

I have done this so many times before. Why should this analyst be different? On the other hand, why should he not? There are the smile, the dark circles, the penetrating eyes, his slenderness, which makes me feel tenderly toward him, it couldn't be easy to be a man that size growing up in this culture. I too have not found it easy to grow up in this culture. Maybe he will, maybe he won't, maybe he will understand.

Of course, things could go wrong between us. I might not be able to bring all of myself into this analysis. Perhaps this analysis too will go along on a certain track with me in the sidecar, carried along by the momentum of the analytic vehicle, but not really in the driver's seat. Perhaps, too, this analyst might not share Fliess's view of innate bisexuality. He might try to talk me into giving up the formerly repressed half that has now been offered a chance, during the last five or six years, to thrive. Perhaps he will have conventional analytic opinions about the way my father, being absent, failed to seduce me into an attraction to men. Therefore, I will have to relate once again the wild nights of my heterosexual experience. He might not believe I regard my bisexuality as an achievement, not something I wish to undo. He might not know what disintegration means.

While I am telling him about my recent troubles, I notice that my intensity, which grows as I am talking, is alarming to him. He sits further back in his chair, making space between us. His eyes seem to retreat, sinking back into shadow. Therefore, another danger. Perhaps this man will not be able to hold my intensity, perhaps it will seem incongruous to him, or he might end up being attracted to it, and thereby lose objectivity, or deprive me of my place here as a suffering subject, who does not want the analyst to be attracted to me although of course I do.

The familiar discourse is taking place, the wonderful unfolding of the analytic story, themes clicking into place, patterns emerging, meanings rising to the surface, feelings gathering. Then too, our conversation has already given rise to that other track of analytic consciousness, on which I am minutely studying the relationship between us, taking notes, adding up impressions. If he is doing the same with me, we are sitting in this room, each in our comfortable chair, involved in a twofold act of concentration.

By now, I have spent most of my adult life in psycho-analysis. I am familiar with the analytic situation, the analyst's calm, interpretive curiosity, which has been present in all three analytic experiences. I expect the absence of judgment, which allows the self to explore its various nefarious inclinations. I value the listener's quiet, which is like no other, being more vast, more dense, more resonant than other silences, more like the silence that occurs between musical notes, defining them, stringing them together. There is intimacy, which one fears and desires, which cannot be avoided because of the fifty minutes during which so little or so much will be said. This is a structured situation, it has its regular comings and goings, one knows what to expect from it. This is helpful to a self that is sometimes at the edge of chaos. Then too, the analyst sometimes seems a person who has accomplished the impossible, an integration of self that therefore might be possible for one too. And there are the interpretations, those comments that will offer the clarity that brings relief from conflict. All this is familiar.

Nevertheless, psychoanalysis has changed over the years since Freud invented it. It might be possible to see, in my three analytic experiences, the developmental movement that has taken place within psychoanalysis itself. This is perhaps no accident. Each analyst has sent me on to the next, knowing the new analyst's orientation.

To begin with, there was Freud's scientific allegiance. A man of his age, he believed in truth and the possibilities of discovering it. That meant the analyst's capacity to know the patient's struggles better than the patient, to clarify these conflicts through definitive interpretations based on psychoanalytic insights that had uncovered the fundamental laws of the human psyche.

When I went into psychoanalysis the first time I still believed in truth, in the possibilities of discovering it. My analyst did not awaken me from this illusion. The stories that emerged about my childhood seemed accurate constructions and reconstructions of childhood events that had actually taken place. Knowing the past led to freedom of choice, choice led to the exercise of will, will buttressed the ego defensively against raids from the untamable id.

Of course, no psychoanalyst has ever told me her orientation. Nevertheless, when you sit with someone for many years, even if she is largely silent, you begin to form impressions of what she is all about. Perhaps my second analyst was interested in the adaptive (rather than purely defensive) mechanisms of the ego. She might have been interested in the relations between the ego and its social world of meaningful others; perhaps she cared theoretically as much for this social network as for the inner world created by repressions. If so, she would have been working with analytic ideas evolved since Freud, modifying drive theory, adding twists and turns to the stark, oedipal dramatics.

More recently, psychoanalysis has entertained a wild

gathering of subjectivists, hermeneuts and construc-
tivists, who often seem to have shrugged off truth as
beyond the pale, would be willing to construct just about
any story. This lot, with which I identify myself, has been
shaped by trends in the general culture which go by the
name of postmodernism, deconstruction. Under these
influences, analytic theory has moved from truth to construction, from knowledge to a good tale, from objectivity to the fully realized subjective dread of not yet knowing, not yet naming. Where before the analyst sat
enthroned in scientific objectivity, observing the know-
able subject on the couch, analytic chambers these days
are filled with two subjectivities, with partial knowings,
some good guesses, along with minutely observed interactions taking place right now, in this room, between
these two people. As for truth, according to this view, it
holds a close affinity with fictions, carrying ambiguities,
sustaining multiple meanings, through which a fertile,
contradictory, sometimes singular, sometimes multiple
self is said to derive, sometimes with a core, sometimes
without.

So here I am, a few weeks into the third analysis,
stretched out on the couch, no longer a believer in truth,
a self that has lived and died numerous times, ready to
enter discourse at the sharp edge of the analytic world,
where interpretations will be probing, tentative; where
transference will take place and be examined; where
countertransference will be known to exist, although (as

it turns out) it will not be openly discussed, until it erupts into the analysis shortly before the analysis comes to an end.

How am I doing? Not bad, for an experiment. I've been pleased to discover a good old dialectic tension between wildness and reason, as if this writing really were capable of changing me psychoanalytically, as I charge along. Of course, I don't refer here to psychoanalysis as a scientific instrument, a flawed objectivity studying its own flawed nature. Freud, if you ask me, was one of our culture's great imaginative writers. That may be the reason he envied Dostoyevski, to whom he peremptorily denied the epileptic diagnosis, to relocate him in the company of hysterics, among whom Freud counted himself. Like Dostoyevski, Freud knew how to lay out a good story, to string it together with a mere handful of themes, a compelling plot line, a mysterious unknown then violently unearthed by dogged perseverance.

Anyone who thinks Freud will be driven from his place in the history of thought under the recent barrage of scientific exposures probably has never fallen under the spell of the literary Freud. Who could forget the Rat Man, with his obsessive fantasies of self-torture? Dora, refusing to enjoy Herr K's embraces, walking out on the analysis with Freud, is another of the great characters of the early twentieth century. Psychoanalysis is dead? Long live psychoanalysis. It has that cunning, evolutionary, revisionist tendency of all great bodies of thought: it is capable of infinite adaptation to the changing conditions of knowledge. Psychoanalysis can transform itself so completely its lineage (what it was, what it has since become) can scarcely be traced, while it goes right on calling itself psychoanalysis. And why not? In this respect, it behaves just like the self it was invented to discover, a shape changer if ever there was one. Why, even I think of myself as a psychoanalyst.

So where am I? Somewhere near the beginning of my third psychoanalysis. This one will last for eight years. The analyst has nothing much to say about bisexuality. Occasionally he corrects a creeping one-sidedness that comes upon me at times of high rhetoric. He appears to approve of the tense struggle to hold opposites together, makes note of any statement that implies a choice would have to be made between polarities, uses the words "male" and "female" with audible concessions to their cultural construction.

The third analyst also has an unusual gift. He can evoke the feeling states of a very young child. You tell him things other people have not been able to hear, he knows exactly what to make of them. He has studied infants, written about them, expanded the psychoanalytic conception of what infants feel, think, do. I have admired the emphatic tenderness of his descriptions, which make visible a world of infant possibility only mothers have known until now. You are in the room with him, stretched out at your full five feet four and a half inches, when suddenly it is no longer you but a small child who is there, even the child's body is there, its little legs, its tiny fists, its mouth that can never get enough of anything. This living sense of the small child you once were seems to have been sensually preserved along with the other bodies that have grown up, treelike, concentrically, around it. I am now involved in a psychoanalytic process that eases itself back beyond the verbal organization of experience, to the earliest bodily sensations from which a tiny, emergent self has been shaped.

Language is going to find itself in trouble when it attempts to record this experience. Nevertheless, it is clear that the third analyst has a remarkable capacity to place himself tenderly, knowingly, in relation to the tribulations of a little child. He does this in part with his voice, which is calm, steady, infinitely patient, as if nothing can shock him, take him by surprise, surpass his familiarity with it. In his presence, whatever had formerly seemed bizarre can now be given a name, a shape, a definition. Sometimes he can receive a child who has no language but the body. Therefore, through the body it rehearses its griefs, its uncertainties; these are spoken in sensations traveling along the surface of its skin, through mounting nameless tensions that rise and break just at the edge of its ill-conceived boundedness.

In time, one comes to understand how this body-self has its distinctive concerns, not like those of selves that will form later. Being tiny, not yet having ordered the world with language, making no absolutely clear distinction between inside and outside, this body-self seems to flow along in bundles of sensations, through rushes, retreats, the rocking of regular rhythms, heartbeats perhaps, suckings, the throbbing of blood clocking its way through the veins.

These sensations, which flow in and out of the analytic session, are the body's small universe, its little world of self. Gradually, from this sensory ground there arises a surface, which may in time become a circumference that suggests the beginnings of a boundary, holding the self together, defining an inside.

I, who suffer from a feeling that I can come to pieces, make sense within this infantile world. When I feel that I could spill out of myself, that is perhaps the experience of a small being cast back so far into its origins one can scarcely as yet speak of a mother. She who will later become mother exists only as sensation forming along a surface, as softness, hardness, warmth, absence.

Over time it seems possible that the anxieties from which I suffer, the periods of profound panic, have their origin in this world. Back here, we are able to imagine the unthinkable anxiety of the child not sufficiently held by a mothering presence. Better yet, we can name the panic states during which the little one threatens to thaw into a formlessness, to dissolve into its own disintegration.

I have been told that my mother was very depressed when I was born. Later, after my sister died, her depression deepened. As an infant, I was covered in eczema, which can now be thought of as a second skin, an attempt (along with scratching and tearing at the skin) to define a surface, so that the boundary of this surface can keep me from spilling out.

I have no trouble imagining small babies felt this way. I have known these sensations (they are very frightening before they are named) repeatedly during my wakeful nights. If I endured panics and terrors of this type as a tiny child, these states of alarm may have entwined themselves with an emerging self, a flawed entity shaped around a core terror of dissolution. Here were formed the snags and tears in the self, the places a stitch had been dropped during the self's early knitting, holes that perhaps cannot be repaired, no matter how dense the analytic texture.

Nevertheless, these researches into the origins of the self define a new analytic experience. They give me the impression that a relentlessly hidden self-experience has now allowed itself to be known. Being known, having received names, having been separated out into discrete sensations, the global terror of these experiences may now have a chance to abate. The shy self, formerly visited by nameless terrors, indescribable raptures, has now been able to locate itself in a body; it is held in the analysis itself, in the analytic sessions, in the infinite calm of this man's voice. The shy self can now say, "I am here, right here in this body with its sensations, which are my sensations, which are no longer the visitations of unknown, terrible forces. This is me, I can't fall out of myself, this body won't split apart or fall forever, I have a location in my own flesh." The analyst has become a floating, hovering, scarcely placed, palpable presence. This presence carries a sense of protectedness, of being watched over, which comes with me at times even when I am not in the analytic room. Now, late at night or in the late afternoon, when the panics start up again, they are met by his presence, as if he has become part of me, can protect me against myself even from a distance, has found a home in me, from which it will not be possible for the dread of sleepless nights to dislodge him.

I am happy to have these experiences with the third analyst. I know now why I have carried on my analytic work so doggedly for close to a quarter of a century. I have been trying to name these states, in which the self imperfectly formed itself during its unguarded beginnings. If this is not a core, it is at least an experience early enough to satisfy my need for origins. I have kept at my analytic work for close to a quarter of a century because I have been looking for the kind of listening this man practices, in which the preverbal finds a language for itself, a communication through bodily sensations that are meaningful to the other.

The man who has made this possible has helped me

weave a fine mesh of self-enclosure around my formerly skinless sense of self.

Sometimes, a bit later in the analysis, I have the fantasy that I am walking around holding hands with my analyst. It is a comradely, protected feeling, such as I may have had as an older child going through the Bronx park with my father.

So why did this extraordinary psychoanalytic experience end badly? Why did this analysis, which unearthed an original self terror, far back beyond the death of my sister, come to a bad end? This analysis also redeemed my father from the absence in which he was supposed (in both earlier analyses) to have existed. According to the third analyst, my father was an intimate part of my childhood, but forbidden to me by my mother's jealousy of our relationship. In my dreams, my father now came back from the dead, wearing his old leather jacket, no longer the hated gobbler of my mother and sister. In dreams, in waking thoughts, in ghostly images that fade the instant one becomes aware of them, the analyst and the father seem to flow together, their patience, their gentleness, the clarity of their thought, now make them indistinguishable from one another. Because my father has come back to me, because the analyst has found a place in me, because I live in a body that cannot come apart, the world looks different to me. I no longer lose myself crossing a familiar street. I don't think

I will fall off the edge of the world. If the world suddenly came to an end a step or two from where I am standing, the father-analyst would hold on to me. I can now (occasionally) drift into sleep because the analyst-father in his leather jacket is standing there, ever watchful, beside my bed.

The shy self, formerly excluded from analytic discourse, has been able to bring its prelinguistic mysteries into the analytic chamber. Because of this, the shy self loves the analyst, wants to sit on his knees, curl up in his arms, rest her head against his analytic shoulder.

Why therefore the dramatic ending? To answer this question I have had to stop writing for days. During that time I lay on my bed, wandering about through the interior world psychoanalysis has helped me create. This world is by now a fairly large terrain, a landscape that moves on in seemingly endless stretches from primeval formations to a sophisticated, urban architecture of the self. There are memories in here, cloud formations of intense feeling states, the fossil traces of all previous relations. I have also stored up in here the fragments of my experience with culture. Musical phrases, lines from great poems, the stories of characters I have taken to heart have been given a place in this interior self-fabric. Intricate theories kick around in here too, although in this world they are not taken very seriously. Pride of place goes to vivid relivings of past events, which arise spontaneously as one settles into this interiority. If I had to name the single accomplishment for which I am most grateful to psychoanalysis, it would be the existence of this teeming, fecund inner world. Because of its ability to create this world for its analysands, out of emptiness, undifferentiation, vagueness, terror, psychoanalysis will have (I believe) a lasting place among the major achievements of our culture.

But this is not going to be a discourse on gratitude.

Here, therefore, a wish to stop writing. A sudden downpour of distraction. The dropping of a hot cup of tea, which makes a mess of the few notes I made during my interior sojourn. Now I am left to my memory of my memories, an increasingly fallible guide. It's always like that. You come back full of insight and understanding, all caught up in those sudden quick snatches of surmise. Writing then becomes a matter of fadings, darkenings, the tangibles getting lost, things slipping away, the newly grasped falling back into the elusive. No one to blame for this state of affairs. One just keeps plodding forward.

The analyst once referred to my love for music as my ability to get myself into a trance state. When I listen to music I become capable of a highly focused concentration that makes it possible for me to detect musical subtleties for which I am not musically trained. I cultivate this hearing because I want to know as much about music as possible. Nevertheless, the analyst seemed to regard my musical listening as a way of avoiding anxiety, insulating myself from the demands of the real world.

We discussed this disagreement, the analysis flowed on. My memory, however, tucked the misunderstanding away, as if some essential core of the self had been snubbed. Of course I know these misunderstandings happen all the time, the analyst was not to blame. But memory did not forgive him.

So how did this lead to an ending?

During my recent interior foragings I have also found other such instances of feeling snubbed. Apparently this had not happened to the infant self, the body-being emerging from its sensations. For those experiences before language the analyst had an unerring intuition. Perhaps it did not come along with him as the analysis moved on, bringing him face to face with the contemporary woman whose excitable, passionate nature eluded him?

Here a caution must be sounded. This feeling, that my nature is too passionate to be understood by a man, may well have grown up straight out of my childhood, when I experienced my mother and myself as a hurricane of intensity, both of us far too elemental, too primitive, for the gentle, thoughtful man who was my father.

The third analyst can point out this element of transference in my response to him. Still, I wonder. Maybe the analysis came to a bad end because there really was something about my nature that eluded the understanding of the third analyst?

For instance, he seemed unfamiliar with writing that took place through ecstatic outpouring of words, states of overexcitement that led, he believed, to exhaustion. In these overexcitements he detected hidden resistances, anxieties about writing, conflicts that had never come to the surface. An analyst deserves a good hearing when he has helped one to feel settled in oneself. I, for instance, was with every year a stronger, more coherent self. That meant: less turbulent relationships, enduring friendships, a growing body of written work, a reputation as a good analytic listener to people in trouble. Of course I listened.

Nevertheless, the self had recorded another snub. Apparently, it regarded itself as fundamentally a creature of ecstasies and excitements, which it had no wish to renounce. It couldn't figure out why the analyst knew nothing about the sublime power of these states, through which the self achieved its enduring transformative momentum.

The analyst wondered why I did not make better use of footnotes in my writing. He seemed to imply that my reading had influenced me more than I knew, that what I regarded as original thoughts were in fact derived from other, influential thinkers of my culture.

Footnotes, I agree, might deserve an entire analysis of their own. Perhaps another twenty-five years might profitably be given over to the question of footnotes. Although I have already explained this to the analyst, it can't hurt to make note of it here again. I don't make use of footnotes because of the erratic way in which I read, at a furious speed, gobbling things up, instantly forgetting them. Of course my reading influences me, ideas get reworked as my own, become part of the primordial batch from which later writing emerges in that torrent from which the analyst had thought it might be better to protect myself. But footnotes for a torrent?

Of course, none of these matters are significant in themselves. I probably poured tea over my notes because I am ashamed of them. One would far rather concentrate on the great analytic sweeps and discoveries, the harmony that arises, often late in a session, as the room is getting dark, when some part of the self that has long been silent suddenly, because of this man's presence, finds itself in words. But memory has thrown together a bunch of slights in which the self felt misvalued. In this work of preservation, memory is probably trying to come up with an answer to a mystery.

Why, after all, did an analytic experience of such depth end badly?

All of psychoanalysis is an effort to explain mysteries: tics, stomach pains, nightmares, the unforgiving passion for a stranger glimpsed from a bus window. At the start of a psychoanalysis one is filled with certainty that mystery can be fathomed. But in time the effort to explain mystery predictably meets with problems. The tic relocates itself, the pain settles in the lower back, the nightmare restrings itself, the explanations keep changing, the mystery endures.

During my first two analyses, even for a few years during the third, I was steady in my conviction. If I could manage to suffer, cast down understanding into darkness, I would get to the place from which panics, terrors, pains, anguish, self-doubt, fragmentation had once originated. That was the promise of psychoanalysis as I had imagined it years before, crossing the street to the first analyst's house. Because I believed in the relief of symptoms, even more in the virtues of self-knowledge, I never doubted the efficacy of psychoanalysis. If I suffered, that meant I hadn't got to the bottom of things. If symptoms changed form, that meant there were unknown conflicts, a still deeper subterranean world to explore. If my late afternoons now have become a time of exhaustion, loss of hope, when I frequently have to take to bed simply to endure the mental anguish that lasts often for hours, that means I have to try harder to give the anguish a name.

I don't know why I suddenly (nothing is sudden in the life of the mind) began to doubt this psychoanalytic promise. Perhaps I had spent so long, at such depth, with such intricacy of naming, that I had come to believe I had a right to suffer less. (The demand not to suffer tends to be viewed psychoanalytically as regressive.)

Maybe I wanted explanations to hold up better, for the analytic interpretations to remain constant, instead of shifting and changing from one analysis to the next, from year to year, while the bottom of it all proved to be end-lessly recessive.

Maybe, far off, an unthinkable thought had long since begun to create itself. Perhaps I could persist with analytic work for another twenty years and never manage to overcome the ever-changing symptoms of mental dis-tress that followed a by now inevitable psychoanalytic pattern: the symptom abates, a new self-experience is launched, a new, shadowy realm is created outside the analysis, perhaps excluded from it, until it erupts into the analysis, bringing the analysis to an end. Perhaps my anguish of the late afternoons, when the world seemed to darken, become strangely lifeless, as if I were the last person alive on a dying planet, this new, unexplained dis-tress marked the spot where a still-unknown could not enter the analysis, even after the shy self had made its way in.

One day on the way to an analytic session I suddenly realized how angry I was at psychoanalysis, at the analyst, at the uncertainty of my mental future, which might con-tain new panics, undiscovered fragmentations, tremen-dously troubled afternoons, no matter how long I hung around.

A troubling thought, an eruption.

Other thoughts swim up out of the unthinkable.

Perhaps I had been conducting my own analysis all along, struggling, descending, casting light, naming, on a self-journey that had very little to do with Freudian thought? Perhaps I had been working with self-stuff that had remained perfectly unknown to my analysts?

I suppose, over the analytic years, a rather stubborn self had formed itself, with its own notion of what things meant to it. If it spoke about mystical states, it didn't much care for the analyst's attempt to make these out to be derivatives of childhood experience, without simultaneously understanding them as the exquisite poetics of a maturing self. Spillings and splittings and disintegrations, yes! But the self in its rapturous intuition of something far more deeply interfused? This did not seem a matter on which the psychoanalytic understanding of childhood had much to offer. Could it be that psychoanalysis, invented to study the self in its most hidden gestures, has managed to ignore passion, love, ecstatic states, mystical intuitings—the self's most mysterious shadow play?

These delicate matters have come in for analytic discussion through the eight years of the third analysis. They have been gone over in detail, we are both mature people, we understand by now that differences are tolerable, one survives them. It has become clear that the analyst has nothing to say against my bisexuality. He may not celebrate it as I do, but he is not trying to get rid of it. I have not had to produce Freud or Fliess or the early, theory-making years of the psychoanalytic movement. Little by little, nevertheless, my memory has gathered up moments in which the third analyst seems to have been speaking to someone who is not quite me. As if there were another Kim Chernin, a woman of his own making, lying next to me on the couch. There is nothing much wrong with the analyst's version, it just does not match up fully with my own.

Here, of course, we have entered a subtle, devilish domain, which will plunge us right into the hot, contemporary debates about psychoanalysis. These involve the problem of knowing. For instance, it could be that I attribute to the analyst my own sense of an incorrect version of myself. Perhaps this inaccurate version is really of my own making, a sort of shadowy me I believe he has invented because I cannot live with the implications this other version might contain.

Tricky stuff.

There does not seem to be a clear way to sort these things out. Because we both recognize this, the analysis has therefore advanced to an awareness of a necessary ambiguity. On the ground of that unknowing, that suspension of knowledge, the third analysis must now proceed. I am talking about a very subtle, sophisticated man. Although I can know him (perhaps) only through transference, I have formed an impression of him over the years. He seems to me a highly intellectual person, of considerable wisdom, whose wisdom has been derived from profound thought. I don't have the impression he has lived a great deal all over the world, in and out of relationships, traveling about in foreign places, struggling with strange languages, as I have. I always picture him on vacation with his wife and family sitting under an umbrella next to a swimming pool, or on the beach, reading. This may be a transposed image of my father, or it may be an intuition about the way the third analyst spends his vacation.

How am I to know? Shall I trust his sense that I know him through the construction I have made of him in the image of my father? Or shall I trust what seems to me a growing knowledge of him, the man?

At moments of uncertainty I always go back to memory. What does memory have to say? Volumes! The third analyst has always regarded my love affairs as addictions, not as the transformational events I think they have been. Trance states, addictions, excitable writings, the lack of footnotes. All this adds up to a person who is not exactly the person I make of myself. Am I supposed to change from the person he thinks I am? Would that be considered analytic progress? How can I change if I am, to begin with, not this person? Maybe I shall end my days in a storm of passionate states, falling in and out of love, an old woman still writing day and night, losing track of time, a somewhat wild, eccentric creature wandering out to the edge of my known world, where mystical thoughts are blasted at me.

Tricky stuff. A quicksand of subjective possibilities.

How can I know if it is the analyst, or I myself, who has taken against this vision of my future? He believes in his neutrality with respect to a choice like this. My memory has written him down as having a temperament of his own, which knows very little about passionate states, is likely therefore to come up with interpretations that reflect his temperamental leanings.

For instance, I am an outsider. As a Jew, a woman, the daughter of immigrants, a child of the far left, raised in a poor neighborhood in the Bronx, I seem to have been born to my outsider status. What can he, a man who has followed a more conventional path, from prep school to college, to Ivy League medical school, to advanced analytic training in New York, know about an outsider? He seems to feel I might do more to integrate myself in more conventional institutions. Perhaps this will relieve the anxiety I still so often feel. Does he think I should go back to graduate school, get an advanced degree in clinical psychology? He seems to think this is what I wish for myself, although the wish remains hidden. But whose wish is this? And, even if it is mine, is this a wish I wish to follow? Would the conventional, institutional path be the best for me? Or would I do better to stick with my outsider ways, for all the anguish and uncertainty, sleepless nights, unsettled future this might well cause me?

A born outsider discussing her future with an analyst.

If he is no longer an authority, not capable therefore of an irreproachable objectivity, we can imagine that he will be made uneasy, on behalf of his analysand, by those things that make him uneasy for himself. He, with his well-deserved, hard-earned, institutional attachments, would probably not be comfortable in life as an outsider.

Analysts, even when deprived in theory of absolute authority, carry considerable authority. It hangs on, long after it has been theoretically dismantled, in a tone of voice, the practiced mastery of silence, the timing of comments, the serene certainty with which interpretations continue to be made. As it happens, I too for a time took to the straight and narrow. I went back to graduate school, received my degree in clinical psychology. Therefore, today I am faced with a question: would I have gone back to school if I had not been in that particular analysis? Does this decision reflect the analyst's influence on me, perhaps against my own bent? Or have I been brought through my conversations with him to these more conventional choices as an expression of my own deeper desires, formerly hidden from me until he discovered them to me?

Who knows? What is known? Does he know better than I do? Do I know what I think I know? Can I trust my perceptions? Are my perceptions of him necessarily transferences? Is my feeling of uneasiness in the analytic process the sign of an internal conflict? Or is there something, analytically speaking, going wrong?

These questions, which arise in the most advanced analytic relationships of our time, can never be answered. They are the psychoanalytic ambiguities with which the analyst and analysand must come to live. If the analyst has lost the authority of knowing Freud conferred upon him, what makes his opinion more compelling than that of his analysand? In the dialectical tension of this uncertainty the third psychoanalysis now turns dramatic.

Certainly the analyst occasionally makes mistakes. Years ago, he had told me that a woman with whom I had fallen in love would always have other lovers in her life. If I have chosen her for distance, in order to feel through repeated loss of her an enhanced desire, I should (in his opinion) face this squarely. I have chosen someone who will never fully be able to return my love. This has been a clearly stated analytic position. But then the woman breaks up all previous relationships, leaves Paris, moves to Berkeley (this is a good seven years ago now) to live with me.

Memory has set this down emphatically as an instance in which I knew more than the third analyst knew.

So now, in addition to other accomplishments, the writing, the friendships, my work as an analytic listener, I have also achieved a long-term relationship. My self has acquired what is thought of as structure. Yes, I know by now I won't disintegrate. My self is too stubborn to come apart. It won't dissolve into a dew, fall into shapelessness. It still has its bad nights, those late afternoons, but it has figured out ways to get through them.

Better yet, it has developed a certain cunning about itself. It takes pride in this cunning. When this self falls into its most fundamental gesture, it finds itself a sly, honest creature, with fiercely glittering eyes. In this self-portrait, it has inscribed a defiant resistance to the claim that anyone can know it better than it knows itself. The shy self has succeeded in entering the analytic process. The mature woman who has grown up angry, rebellious, defiant, headstrong, confident, self-fashioning out of that lost child has trouble getting in. She resents this.

This will lead to a bad analytic end.

Outsiders are an ungrateful bunch, they can't be confined by theoretical systems, after a while, no matter how hard they have been trying to fit in somewhere, they inevitably grow rebellious. This fretfulness will probably be interpreted as a sign that the analysand has not yet been able to grow up, make a reasonable peace with authority, adapt to the limitations other people have accepted.

Outsiders cherish an illusion: they are capable of ideas that could not occur within the traditional institutes. Institutes cherish an illusion: they have already thought of everything the outsider can think up. Outsiders pride themselves on their originality. Their ideas have come at white heat out of their own experience. Institutes remind them: these ideas have already been formulated by other people.

When you are studying psychoanalysis on your own, reading whatever you can, attending public lectures, forming individual study groups, you will probably end up consulting with trained analysts about your clients, no matter how much an outsider you think you are. There is an unofficial, often highly rigorous training of the outsiders, who form an unacknowledged circle of their own around the official institutes. In San Francisco recently, some of these unofficial folk have formed a new psychoanalytic institute for the more radical education and training of psychoanalysts. This new institute has become a second circle around the traditional group, thus driving the outsiders into a third circle.

This is as it should be. Taken together, all three circles preserve an essential aspect of the original psychoanalytic impulse. We today know psychoanalysis as an international movement, holding congresses in Amsterdam and Paris, sponsoring prestigious, scholarly journals, to which the International and American Institutes of Psychoanalysis contribute. As a movement, psychoanalysis tends to be hierarchical, highly organized, the preserver of a (near)-century-old tradition of training and thought.

But there was a time when the first international congress of psychoanalysis in Salzburg consisted of forty-two participants, twenty-one of them from Vienna. Freud spoke nonstop for over four hours about one of his clients, who has since come to international prominence as the Rat Man. C. G. Jung was there and Karl Abraham, presenting a paper on autoeroticism, a concept that may have been originally inspired by Jung.

Things being named for the first time, discoveries being made, excited folk gathered to exchange excitements. This spirit probably lives on in second-circle psychoanalysis, at the fledgling institutes, where the courses and reading lists are more precariously at the cutting edge than they would likely be in more established places.

And then of course there are the psychoanalytic outsiders. The people who carry on the line of the obscure Freud, with his handful of colleagues, meeting on Wednesday evenings in Vienna before psychoanalysis had achieved international recognition. If something as shocking as the idea of infantile sexuality is going to show up again, it might first have to make its appearance among people who think odd thoughts without institutional sanction. When someone writes the hidden homoerotic history of psychoanalysis, it will probably not be read for the first time at a formal meeting of any psychoanalytic institute.

(Unfortunately, I have no time to pursue this fascinating topic here. I can mention only in passing the father-son homoerotics that accompanied Freud from Breuer to

Fliess right down into his relationship with Jung. Sometimes, I imagine presenting a psychoanalytic paper that asks the fundamental question whether the driving force of the early psychoanalytic movement was a barely sublimated homoerotic yearning. Certainly that would account for the tensions and jealousy, quarrels, factions, and defections that marked the urgent early days of psychoanalytic thought. Perhaps, in its contempt for the outsiders, institutional psychoanalysis is to this day fleeing from its own unanalyzed father-son erotics?)

Third-circle psychoanalysis is a world unto itself. If you keep attending weekly lectures, taking weekend workshops, participating in advanced courses, dropping in for lectures at the various graduate schools, you will soon become familiar with this extended psychoanalytic family. The very same people (many of them women) will show up for every psychoanalytic luminary who comes to town. This is a wide-open world, in which no one has had to declare an ideological allegiance. Debates spill out into the foyer, surround the table spread with cookies and paper coffee cups. In between lectures, debates, more formal gatherings, there are small psychoanalytic study groups that meet regularly, sometimes for decades. There are the hot topics, the current issues, the new discoveries, the latest theory turning over the older theories, which manage somehow to get back on their feet. New journals and newsletters arrive in the mail, new graduate schools spring up practically overnight, schools and schisms form before your eyes. This is education the way I like it, fiery, talmudic, democratic.

As part of my participation in this third world, I had been working with people who were having troubles. I also had been consulting about my work with analysts of every persuasion. This somewhat romantic procedure, this peripatetic psychoanalysis, suited me well. It reminded me of students in the nineteenth century, traveling from university to university to attend lectures by the masters. I didn't want to get caught up in any particular school. I wanted an ecumenical education. Every theory (I thought) must contain an authentic piece of autobiography, would therefore be relevant to one of my clients, sooner or later.

Of course, I didn't always think this way. At first, when I started listening psychoanalytically to people, I thought I was supposed to tell them what things meant. They had dreams, associations to their dreams, I had the dreams' meanings. They had memories, I reconstructed their childhoods. This can be very soothing to people who are feeling troubled. Most folk like to believe someone knows more than they do, has a grasp of how things work, knows the laws that govern the psyche.

One day, I suppose in a process similar to what was taking place in my own psychoanalysis, I started to wonder: How the hell do I know what this man's dream means? What do I know about this woman's childhood? Repression notwithstanding (who says there is such a thing as repression?), they probably know a lot more about these things than I do.

What does it mean to *train* a person to be present with another person for fifty minutes? Does being present with another have to become a highly specialized act? Formal? Practiced? Does this need for formality suggest one can only have a relationship with one's own unconscious through the authoritative mediation of another person? For instance, why do psychoanalysts wear suits and ties and their equivalent? The best way to practice psychoanalysis is in a sweatsuit.

I know, I'm getting carried away. These must be the things I wanted to say to the third analyst. Consequently, they have to be forgiven a hint of wildness, a polemical ring. They'll calm down again.

On the other hand, why should they? I am just about to make a public declaration of my psychoanalytic anger, to pronounce myself a perennial outsider, whose train will never arrive at the psychoanalytic station on time. (Go on, dare to say it.) The third analysis ended as it did because the analyst was too conventional to understand an irreproachably unconventional, hotheaded, stubborn, rebellious woman.

There's more to it than that. There's always more to it. Explanations I could offer, stories I could unfold, to account for the coming end of (my) psychoanalysis. Some of these stories I have decided to keep private.

Even writers have a right to privacy, even when their readers have been cast in the role of psychoanalyst. Why should I trust my readers with a full confession? Even psychoanalytic patients, in this most recent, revisionary, liberal phase of psychoanalysis, have been granted rights to a private world, secrets they never surrender. This was said to me by the third analyst, who had heard it from an old man who had been an analyst for so many years even the analytic institutes were forced to overlook his unconventionality. During a period of (my) outspoken despair with psychoanalysis, the third analyst suggested I consult with this man about my clients. (This consultation, which lasted for many years, was originally going to become the central panel of my triptych. If this experiment in free association goes on much longer, it will soon become a book of its own.)

This old man was then in semiretirement, living in an obscure, lovely town near the Richmond oil refineries, on the wind-fresh side, in a house that looked out toward San Francisco, over the bay. There is an old tiered garden around his house, it descends all the way to the water. In the old days, before pollution, his wife used to go swimming from their front steps. When you first walk in there, off the street, the wind comes up fresh and it seems as if you are standing on the deck of a ship. He was a graduate of the Washington School of Psychiatry and the Washington Psychoanalytic Institute. He had been an analysand of Harry Stack Sullivan and Frieda

Fromm-Reichman, had become their colleague. He had written some eighty-five papers about his work with psychotic patients in long-term therapy. He had been the director of the Austen Riggs Center in Stockbridge, Massachusetts (a famous treatment facility for psychotics). He had seniority, lineage, institutional recognition, fame. People told stories about him. He had dramatically helped desperately troubled people, whom most other analysts would have considered beyond cure. I knew all this before I went out to see him; it impressed me. I was even more impressed with his underground reputation in the psychoanalytic community. Psychoanalysts went into treatment with him; this was often kept secret. Analysts in training went into treatment with him after they had finished their own training analyses. Senior psychoanalysts went to consult him when they had difficult cases, for which the usual psychoanalytic procedures did not seem appropriate. Yet, somehow, this old man with his impeccable psychoanalytic qualifications had remained an outsider, practicing a line of interpersonal psychoanalysis that had never met with great enthusiasm in the traditional institutes. How am I going to sum up in a few pages the work I did with him?

He changed my life. That's easily said. If I had said it to him, he would have asked how, then waited to hear a detailed answer. I might have said he made me less afraid of the trouble in very troubled people, therefore less afraid of myself. After a time I figured out that he trusted me as a clinician. When clients asked me to bring in a couch, I did so. Little by little, I gave up interpretation in favor of curiosity. I never heard from him a single word of theory or professional jargon, never a story about another person that sounded like any story I had heard before. His reality in the room, the sense of his presence, introduced me to the quality I wanted to bring to my own clients. Because of him I figured out that the training of a psychoanalytic listener must involve the struggle to be oneself in the presence of another person, even against that person's tendency to turn one into someone else, or one's own inclination to play a "therapeutic role." The implications of the interpersonal, as he practiced it, were tough to live up to, easy to slip away from into a professional posture when the going got rough. Words are not going to get it. The man was real (in a way that I had not met with before in a psychoanalyst). In his presence I felt myself become more real, I brought this sense of reality to my clients, who noticed the difference, seemed to relax, expand, open up, find it easier to remember. He had a way of translating the most complex theoretical flights into the language of direct responses. When talking to him, psychoanalytic theory (in which I had been immersed for so many years) came to seem largely irrelevant to the encounter between two people for fifty minutes in a quiet room.

Whenever I drove away from the old man's house, especially during the first few months, I would find myself saying, Yes, this is what I want, this is what I have always wanted. Could an analysis be like this, this real, warm, spontaneous, with a lived profundity rather than a merely analytic depth? I had already figured out that mysteries are not going to give themselves over lightly to explanations. A great teacher will always remain a mysterious presence, precisely because he is so real. He seemed to like people, to welcome them into his presence, without needing to shield himself from them through the precise regulation of rules, times, dates, changes. I felt safe with him, in the way you might feel with a great old rock that knew how to keep on through any weather. One of his psychotic patients had once told him he looked like a cross between Boris Karloff and Abraham Lincoln. He was very tall, somewhat emaciated, stooped, with a fine, square face, blunted features. He communicated a rock-solid sense of what life was all about, as if to say, "Well, it's there, better know it as well as one can, without being too presumptuous about one's knowledge."

After a time, because of my work with him, I began to wonder if the psychoanalytic insistence on transference was a way of dodging the here and now of the psychoanalytic encounter. Could transference be a theoretical loophole for the analyst's slipping out of the relationship, delicately receding from the connection by insisting the relationship is something other than it is because what it is seems too hot to handle? I also began to think of so-called resistance as the analyst's failure to have caught on to the patient's communications, only some of which were verbal.

Not that the old man ever raised these questions himself. They seemed to hang around in the implications of his stories, to come with me after I left, unforgettable precisely because of their ambiguity, which had never been surrendered to the illusion of theoretical clarity. Comments he had made, seemingly in passing, fragments of stories he had told would pop up suddenly during my work with my own clients, as if the old man's wry humor, his penchant for doubting every "truth," had become part of my own listening.

As time went by, I started to love him because he saw no need to explain everything that had taken place during a session, no need to interpret it, not even necessarily to comment on it, if one were able to respond to it directly. The immediate, unmediated give-and-take of something happening now, between these two people—that is what mattered, however much their relationship had been foreshadowed or sometimes carried historical meanings. For him, it seemed, the present reality of two people speaking together was as firmly established as the inevitable waves of projection, fantasy, transference that travel through a relationship.

"Say the obvious," he said to me more than once when certain clients demanded to know why I charged for cancellations.

What was the obvious?

"This is the way you earn your living."

More often than not my clients seemed satisfied with this response, as they had not been with my earlier (often wild) interpretations of their need to challenge the established analytic arrangements, get me to take care of them at my expense, prove their importance to me by putting their needs before my own, etc. Over time my clients and I devised a flexible policy of cancellations, with a certain number of uncharged cancellations (usually three in a year), easygoing substitutions (whenever possible in the same week), paid cancellations (for more than three in a year, when these did not prove to be rearrangeable). There were also exceptions to these categories (emergencies, illness, traffic accidents), I leaving it to the client to determine into which category the cancellation fell. Many clients, for instance, did not think of emergencies, illness, or traffic accidents as a reason not to pay me for a missed session. Others took the opportunity to argue their cause against their perception of my need or their fear of my authority. No one, in the years since we evolved this policy, has taken advantage of this flexible arrangement, probably because it had been worked out with an articulate awareness of the clients' need not to pay for sessions they were unable to attend, my acknowledged need for regularity in the earning of my living.

That may be what the old man meant by "the obvious."

A troubled client who usually came late, then constantly looked over her shoulder to stare at the clock, one day left her jacket in the room after a session. A jacket in the room after a session! This is the opportunity for an interpretive field day. On my way out to Point Richmond to talk to the old man, I ran through possible transference interpretations (client wants more contact with me, wants to stop by at an irregular time to get a glimpse into my personal life, needs to feel that she is special by getting me to talk with her outside of our scheduled time, etc.). Then the inevitable interpretations of resistance (client expresses her ambivalence about our work by leaving part of herself behind, while insisting during the session that she is not coming back next time).

He looked amused when I recited these possibilities, did not actually say we could go on with this exercise until the cows came home, but after a time I fell silent.

He said, "Not everything has meaning."

"Do you mean I don't have to interpret this to her?"

"Some communications," he said, "are complete in themselves. What would you do if you didn't interpret?"

"What would I do? If she wants to pick it up before our next session? I would fold the jacket carefully and put it out on the porch, wrapped in tissue paper."

"Sounds like a thoughtful thing to do. I imagine she would appreciate it."

She did. Or at least that's the impression I got when

she arrived early for the next session, glanced only once or twice at the clock, seemed more relaxed in my presence, made a joke when she left about deliberately forgetting the jacket so she could see me more often.

My friends from the Analytic Institute tell me there are many supervisors who would have recommended engagement rather that interpretation. I can believe this, but have not myself encountered the old man's spirit either in my own analysts or those I have consulted. Larger than life personalities elude language; it tends to reduce them to categorical size so that it can describe them. The old man's wry humor, his consciousness of breaking the rules for the sake of bringing about human connection, his imperturbable sense of what the human response would be in any situation, his vast experience with troubled people, his calm irreverence for doing things by the book, his thorough knowledge of the book, his respect for the inherent capacity of one's clients to forge a personal connection, however damaged in the course of their lives this capacity may have been, taken together these produced an analytic attitude other people advocate but never fully seem to practice.

And then there was the time I danced with my client, a behavior not ordinarily regarded as correct psychoanalytic practice. He was a lonely, shy, sad, inhibited man, approaching sixty, who lived alone in a small town on the South Bay. He did not drive, had no friends, worked in construction during the day, translated Russian poetry at night. In the last years he had been translating the wildly passionate Russian poet Marina Tsvetayeva, with whom (he said) he had fallen in love. If so, she would have been the only love of his life.

He had told me a lot about his childhood in Moscow, where he had been raised from the age of six by a maternal aunt after his mother died of tuberculosis. He had never known his father, who may or may not have been killed in the early years of the Revolution. His life with his aunt had been severe, solitary, tragically uneventful. She never left their small apartment, where they both slept in the single room next to the kitchen. He had a cot, some books, a photograph of Boris Pasternak, a chess set, a few clothes neatly arranged behind a makeshift screen that separated him from the rest of the room. Here he lived, virtually without communication with his aunt, unhappily going and coming from school, where he had made no friends among his schoolmates, getting poor grades, alienating the teachers with his precocious questions, returning home to ignore his homework while he sat brooding over the chessboard, lost in fantasies about the life he would live someday, as a writer in Paris, when he had won the most prestigious literary prize.

His only communication with his aunt took place whenever he moved fast, raised his voice, made a spontaneous gesture. She then, with apparent alarm, would caution him not to exhaust himself, sometimes reaching out to physically inhibit his movement, which she perceived as a danger to his health.. His shyness, inhibition, difficulty communicating, his inveterate solitude, the uneasiness with which he came to talk to me seemed adequately explained by his early history. I was surprised by only one circumstance: the speed, over the first few months, with which he came to tell me his life story, his evident comfort being in the room with me, the absence of tension, anxiety, during the fifty minutes of our conversation. It was he who requested the couch, because it reminded him of the hours he had spent alone during his childhood behind the makeshift screen. One day he explained that he had always imagined talking to someone as he lay there alone, had addressed his thoughts to an imaginary listener, and now felt he had found that listener in me.

Still, the man was painfully awkward, bumped into things when he stepped into the room, seemed visibly anxious about speaking above a whisper, as if he anticipated that I would spring up to actively restrain him. Usually, when I went out to greet him in the waiting room, he was hunched over, face averted, eyes cast down, hands folded between his knees, in the posture of someone who had determined to occupy as little space as possible, with the greatest possible economy of gesture.

One day, however, during our fifth or sixth year of work, when I went out to the waiting room, he was standing in front of the door, intensely excited, his pale eyes full of secrets. The minute we got into the consultation room he blurted out, in a loud, husky voice, "I sent in the translations. I did not tell you this. I sent them, now I have a response, this is a positive response, a very positive response to the Tsvetayeva."

I had never seen my client even the least bit animated before. Perhaps because of this I gave a tiny hop of pleasure, rising up onto the front of my foot. He grabbed my hands. He imitated my little hop. I must have hopped back, irresistibly caught up in his excitement. Then he hopped again, still holding on to my hands, and soon the two of us were hopping together in a small circle.

As soon as he settled himself on the couch, the minute I sat down behind him, I thought, "Oh my god, I have been dancing with my client. I better call the old man." When the session was over I went to the phone. A few minutes later I was on my way to Point Richmond. I was tense and nervous as I told the old man my story. Of course, he had heard me talk many times about the translator who worked as a construction worker. He knew all about his childhood, his solitude, his inhibition. He listened to my account of the little hops that grew into bigger hops that became an ecstatic, celebratory dancing. He didn't seemed impressed or disturbed, he asked how the session had gone, was not surprised that my client had spoken for the first time in an exuberant, loud voice, without attempting to restrain himself. When I fell silent, the old man raised his eyebrows.

"Haven't you been telling me for months that this man had a very inhibiting parent?"

"Is that your way of saying there's nothing wrong with dancing with a client?"

"Well," he said, "it could be he needed an analyst who knew how to dance."

One day I asked the old man if he still considered himself an analyst.

He said, "I *am* an analyst."

"Well," I said, "you are, but that's an evasion."

The next time we talked he told me that he would not have been interested in psychoanalysis if he hadn't met Sullivan, whom some people consider the most significant, least recognized influence on contemporary psychoanalysis.

"What was it about Sullivan?" I asked.

"He spoke about people, not cases."

Speaking about people was what the old man and I did together.

I once told him he was the only real teacher I had ever had.

He said, "What did I teach you?"

Because the question took me by surprise I blurted out, "You taught me to break rules."

This caused a smile. "No," he said after a time. "That wasn't something I had to teach you."

That reminds me of the first time I called him, after the third analyst had given me his name. I had already

164

written to him, received no response. When I got him on the phone he told me he was very busy. I called again about ten days later. I told him I still wanted to consult with him about my clients. Nervously, I said, "I have some very interesting cases."

"I'm not interested in interesting cases," he replied. "I'm interested in good therapy."

"Good therapy is what I want to learn from you."

"Well, I'm busy," he said. "It might be better if I give you the names of some other people."

"I don't want other people. I want you."

I heard what seemed the shuffling of pages. "Do you know my address? When would you like to make an appointment?"

Even as memory, that voice has the power to make me sit up straighter, in whatever posture is right for being true to myself. Had I passed a test? I had referred to the people with whom I was working as "cases." So far as I know, I had never done that before. Probably I had been trying to show off, to make a good impression. He called my bluff. A challenge was set, I had spontaneously reached out to meet it. When I put the phone down I was calm, knowing I had found what I had been looking for. What had I been looking for? Some way to practice psychoanalysis without being confined by psychoanalytic rules. Some way to be fully human with my clients, without feeling that I had betrayed myself as a clinician or let the clients down, or caused a break in a therapeutic frame or a lapse in a neutrality. I wanted someone with whom I could entertain doubts about psychoanalysis, who would do more than pay lip service to the doubts, then go on practicing conventional analysis. I wanted someone who told stories, who did not hold much with theories, who had figured out how to sit in a room with troubled people without making them more uneasy than they already were. But of course I did not know I was looking for these things until I found them.

Then, having found them, years before the third analysis came to an end, that ending became inevitable. My consultation with the old man brought me to a crossroads, where sooner or later I would have to radically choose between the conventional and the authentic. The tensions between them could not be resolved otherwise, by me.

A great teacher teaches you to be yourself. That self may or may not be compatible with traditional formulations. There's no way to know this in the beginning. If you end up learning to be yourself, you may find yourself forever beyond the reach of institutions. You might even turn out to be lonelier than you were, except that you have a self, a good companion.

How did my work with the old man bring my third analysis to a dramatic end? That probably needs a long story rather than an explanation. Here, I make note of a growing underground conflict of loyalty between the third analyst, who was in some ways a highly unconventional thinker, and the old man, who was much more so. Through my work with the third analyst I found myself going back to graduate school, heading out in the direction of the Psychoanalytic Institute. When I told the old man about this intention, he said: "Sure, the Analytic Institute would be happy to have you. As a teacher." The old man, without raising a single, theoretical question, had given me room to doubt the fundamental principles of our work. What do I think about the ending of my third analysis? I think my work with the old man had become the shadowy realm I could not bring with me into analysis. Therefore, sooner or later, an eruption would have to take place, leading to analytic disorder and departure.

It is a late Monday afternoon. There has been heavy traffic. Nevertheless, I am on time for my session, although I have to run from my parking place to the analyst's office.

I begin the session with a sense of fatigue. I am telling the analyst about a teenage girl with whom I have just been working. She persistently asks me trying, difficult, challenging questions. While I am answering them, she stares at me with a stony, suspicious expression, as if convinced that what I am saying is nonsense. Every time I answer a question, she is led to another question, which I try to answer, although her expression grows more grim with each of my attempts.

This sort of question: How will it help her to come every week to speak with me? What difference will it make if she talks about her childhood, since the childhood has passed? How can I know if she is telling the truth? Won't I get only her version, with which her parents would disagree? Why should her symptoms go away because she talks about them?

The analyst points out that I have not interpreted her need to ask these questions, have not pointed out the evident anger they contain. That is true. So far, I have made no interpretations. Although I find these questions exhausting, they seem legitimate to me. If I had dared, I too would have asked them many years ago when I first began analytic work. I don't interpret her need to ask these questions, because I know she will experience any interpretation as an evasion of the answers. I don't know how I know this, but I feel certain that it is so.

Therefore, I disagree with my analyst. I tell him I don't think interpretation would be appropriate at this point. He reminds me of my exhaustion. He says the problem (the need to exhaust me by asking unanswerable questions) cannot be solved from "inside the situation." I have to step outside, interpretively, to return to her the task of answering her own questions.

I disagree.

The silence that rises between us is unpleasant. In it, I am aware that I am going to follow out my own hunch about this young woman, although I cannot yet defend it. Something tells me I must visibly struggle to answer her questions, no matter how long this exhausting procedure lasts. I must struggle to find meaningful answers about fundamental questions for which there really are no answers. She must watch me struggle, come to believe in my sincere efforts to engage her, without evading her challenge. When that process is finished, she will, I believe, have the courage to answer her questions herself.

Because all this is still only an intuition, I cannot make a convincing theoretical defense of my position. The analyst and I disagree about the way this situation should be handled, he has given me advice, I have resolved to do things my own way.

I do not know what he is thinking during our silence. Perhaps he is waiting to see how I respond to our awkward situation, in which, silently, inwardly, I am placing my knowledge and experience of analytic work on an equal footing with his own. Perhaps he will resent me if I go my own way? Perhaps he feels that his opinion has the status of truth, carries authority? I reassure myself: I have trusted him for eight years; difficulties, disagreements have arisen before. They do not bring our relationship catastrophically to an end.

When I am leaving the session, I smile. The smile is returned.

Three weeks later, I rush excitedly into the session. Once again, it is a Monday afternoon. I have just been working with the same young woman, who on this day, after some three or four months of our work together, has hesitantly, gropingly, begun to offer her own, speculative answers to her troubling questions. The suspicious look has gone, the stony expression has given way. She is uncomfortable, she sits straight up in her chair with her hands clenched in her lap, she looks scared but she is speculating, doubting, doubling back, trying again, in the tentative way I have been doing during the last many weeks. After each such attempt, she glances at me with a raw terror. I meet this expression with an encouraging nod, leaning toward her. When she gives up in despair, dismissing the whole attempt with a violent wave of her hand, I pick up where she has left off, groping, tentative, doubling back, coming up with a new surmise, until she joins in again and takes over.

This is still an exhausting process. Nevertheless, I leave the session triumphantly. I drive down the freeway to the peninsula at top speed, race up the stairs to the analyst's office, throw myself on the couch, begin talking in my fast-paced, loud, excitable way.

I have an approach that works. It works for me (I do not like what I have understood to be the interpretation of resistance). It works for the client (she has not felt criticized or evaded by my interpretations). I have my own way of doing things! Instead of commenting on the defense, I have collaborated with it, engaged it, joined in as a full participant, until the young woman has felt safe enough to let it go. Several months into this process, she has come to believe it is possible to answer terrifying, fundamental, challenging questions. She has seen me live through the challenge without falling apart. I have met her on her own ground, where she has been scared, angry, convinced I would let her down. Sooner or later, I feel certain, she herself will tell me the background to this situation. One day she will tell the story of how it has come to be so dangerous to ask questions while yet so impossible, in spite of the evident danger, to let them drop. Then it will be her story, not my interpretation. I shall prefer that. It will mean I have created a listening environment in which the client can figure out what things mean to her. We will still be engaged in the analytic process, but it will be she who has taken up the analytic role. As for me, I will have become the type of listener who prepares the receptive space in which another's voice can find itself. What exactly this listening requires I cannot yet say. But I know it is different than the different kind of listening I have experienced as psychoanalysis.

The analyst is silent. This silence makes me talk faster, more exuberantly, suddenly full of this small miracle of having found my own way as an analytic listener. But now a familiar vehemence is coming into my voice, as if I am trying to convince him. There is a battering quality to my speech. I have begun to doubt myself. Soon, I become convinced I have done something wrong.

Out of his silence, I am spinning a case for my own condemnation.

I too fall silent. The silence is unpleasant, decidedly not the companionable silence in which new thoughts, unexpected memories, tend to emerge.

"You haven't said anything," I say finally, as I sense the session drawing to a close.

"What has there been to say? You haven't been asking for my help."

"There's only something to say when I am asking for your help? Nothing to talk about when I'm feeling great about something?"

Silence.

"I can't tell if you still disagree. I don't know what you think. I took a risk. I tried things my own way. It has worked out wonderfully. Theoretically, you could say I have given up interpretation in order to enter directly into my client's dilemma, to join her in it, become part of it until together we can work our way out of it. Why is there nothing to say about that?"

Silence.

"Are you suggesting I only come here to ask for help? That if I'm not asking for help no discourse is possible between us? That's not the impression I've had. We've talked theory before. What's different this time?"

But this time, our time together had just come to an end.

* * *

What follows will lack the burnished quality of events that come back through old memories. There hasn't been enough time for memory to get to work, heightening where it must, chipping away at the irrelevant. No forgiveness has settled in, it's all too raw. I have achieved no superior state of understanding. This experiment, driven forward by thematically charged associations, cannot hope for a serene self-distance. If I was puzzled then, I am still puzzled. If I was angry then, where should that anger have gone?

During the last three months of the third analysis the analyst and I argue with one another through virtually every session. We disagree about Lacan, for whose language I have always held an intense, personal antipathy. We disagree about the need for interpretation. I speak excitedly about the limits of psychoanalysis, having come to feel during my years of work with the old man that its most fundamental concepts must be called into question. Repression? I'm not so sure it exists. Perhaps people spontaneously begin to remember when they are able to tell their own story by having created the listening environment that is right for them. Resistances? Perhaps they are produced artificially by the interpretive structure of the analytic session, then analyzed as if they belonged inherently to the psyche. Free association? Perhaps it is nothing but an analytic contrivance that had let Freud gather enough case material to translate his self-discoveries into universal theories.

The analyst points out that I am angry at him. I point out that he is angry at me. He does not feel that he is angry. He feels that we have been "playing with ideas." I don't think we have been at play. His statement that my critique of psychoanalysis is thirty-five years old does not sound playful to me.

I know perfectly well these criticisms have been made before. But have their implications been taken in by those who make them, have they revolutionized analytic practice, have they made it possible for the third analyst to imagine his analysand might see what is happening in the analysis more clearly than he does? Because if not, something is wrong. I know we are arguing about something.

At times, these sessions are highly exciting. All the ideas I have been storing up over twenty-five years are getting a chance to emerge. I find myself making loud, outrageous statements. I know the analyst is a sturdy fellow. He will not be offended by my critical ideas. We both know sooner or later an analytic session will bring to light whatever has been crouching in darkness, terrified of exposing itself, afraid to be laughed at, intimidated by anticipations of the listener's angry response. I have spouted heretical convictions before now, literally shaking with alarm until his reasoned, dispassionate engagement has reassured me.

This time, however, something is different. I feel that the analyst is cutting me off, just when I am about to get to something. He seems to fly out against my argument before I have had a chance to formulate it. He interrupts me in my associations to my dreams, is less calm than usual, less reasoned, his arguments seem somewhat heated, as if there is an investment in them I had not perceived before.

One day I come up with the notion that psychoanalysis need not be thought of as therapy, which is a treatment for people who are ill. Psychoanalysis, I have suddenly come to believe, might be moved on to new ground as a noninterpretive art, in which people come to sessions to tell their life stories in a collaborative environment individually crafted to encourage the finding of their own voices. This means one could not work with an established technique, since a technique would be derived from a general understanding, not from the unique encounter between teller and listener. The unique quality of this encounter, the fact that it could therefore not be generalized or repeated, would place this type of psychoanalytic act outside the reach of science. In an exuberant voice, I proclaim the birth of the self through storytelling as the fundamental psychoanalytic act.

After a considerable silence, the analyst points out that I am not the only person who thinks these things. There are narrative schools of psychoanalysis, which have raised similar points. No, I insist, I am after something new, although I cannot yet fully, convincingly state it. Something taking place between the third analyst and me is egging me on into one of my worst traits. If I don't watch out, I will soon be trampling anything anyone else has thought to insist upon my own originality. Any moment now my voice will leap to a higher pitch. I will embark upon ever expanding generalizations. Even the narrative schools listen interpretively. In them too, it is the analyst who puts the final spin on the story, shaping the raw material of the patient's psyche. The narrative schools may have raised the problem of construction rather than truth, of multiple narratives rather than a single, definitive version, but they have not yet turned over to the analysand the full responsibility for evolving her unique story in her own voice.

My voice has taken over the analytic chamber. This voice is not proud of itself, it would prefer dignity, quiet, reason. If this voice could be what it wishes to be, it would calmly search out the small bit of self now lost within the sweeping abstractions. The bit of truth around which a particle of self had just now been forming. There is something almost modest I wish to say about the different ways in which people use the word narrative.

Perhaps I came into the world speaking my own name, a self even before I graduated from the womb, born willful and stubborn, ready for a good fight, knowing perfectly well who was who, while yet enjoying long spells of mystical union sucking at my mother.

Silence.

*　　*　　*

There are many kinds of psychoanalytic silence. In some of them, you fall deeper into yourself, discover the thoughts around the corner, find the exuberance to embrace them. In other silences repetitions seem about to occur, you start to imagine the analyst is listening as some earlier person has done, disapprovingly, with menace. Sometimes, in the silence, you perceive an interaction taking place right here and now, between these two people, one of whom is excited, the other of whom seems to be withholding a response.

But how are you to know what kind of silence this is? Usually, you would lean upon the analyst's more objective sense of what is happening in the session. But what if the analyst has got caught up in something too? Perhaps he himself does not know why he is silent, when he would ordinarily respond. Perhaps he does not realize his response, when he finally makes it, has a cutting, defensive, dismissive edge?

The analyst believes I am unable to experience our discourse as playful because my father was not able to play with ideas. I insist I can tell the difference between play and disputation, between friendly challenge and aggression. My father, I point out, was one of the most playful men I have ever known. The analyst, I say, has always struck me as one of the least playful.

The analyst asks about the reason for my intense anger at him. This is a legitimate question. I am very angry, indeed.

Why am I angry?

He does not listen to me when I am talking. He interrupts me, argues with me, slights my ideas. Granted, they may not be earth-shaking, but they are mine, they are new to me, I am excited about them. Why can't he just leave them alone to let them evolve? For me these thoughts are too new to have become playthings. They have emerged after years of silence, organizing a potentially coherent view out of theoretical fragments. This coming together seems an awesome business to me, which he is misperceiving. I sense the emergence of a new self-configuration, which is taking shape through these wild, excited ideas. Why can't he, who has always been so perceptive, appreciate the meaning of this event for me? Why, I ask repeatedly, does he not realize that he too is angry?

My dreams during this (play) time have become turbulent, the repetitive dream repeats itself now almost every night. I am trying to get to the analytic session, I lose my car, my bicycle, miss my bus, wind up in a strange part of town, a foreign city, am lost, can't speak the language, have no money for a telephone call, rush about desperately, time is passing, I will miss the session.

In one dream the analyst has just performed an abortion. In another, he is a terrorist who has plotted to kill off women one by one on a women's cruise. I recognize the danger, warn the other women, figure out a way to escape.

In another dream a famous movie star with the same name as the analyst is in a country restaurant, eating caviar with feta cheese. Although I have been dream-rushing to my analysis, am once again lost, I stop in to speak with the man. "Oh," I say to him, "I have never seen anyone eat caviar with feta cheese. I am Russian, we usually eat caviar with onion and eggs and sour cream."

The analyst hears in this dream a challenge. I am questioning the star-analyst's authority, claiming a priority of ethnic descent, a superior knowledge. To me, the caviar dream has been marked by a fascination with something new, a desire to know more about it. Because we disagree about the dream's interpretation, the analyst wonders why I am determined to challenge him. I wonder why he needs to impose on my dream a story of his own making.

Every session brings up a new disagreement. We make repeated efforts to understand what is happening. The analyst suggests I am angry at him because I am reliving an old anger at my father, projecting the anger onto the analyst, living through an ancient frustration about not being understood. I tell him he has lost touch with what is happening in our work together. He does not seem to appreciate the developmental movement in which I am involved. He does not seem to recognize his own hostility. He does not seem to realize how the analysis itself is in serious danger.

I run through the dreams again. The analyst as abortionist, the analyst as terrorist, the turbulence of the repetitive dream, in which I try so hard to get to the analysis but cannot make it.

Does the repetitive dream record my resistance? Is that what those repetitive dreams have been driving at all these years? Or has this dream been all along an exasperated commentary on my inability to bring myself into an analytic session, so that I can tell my own story, concoct my own version of myself, claim my own authority for what I know?

If these analytic sessions are playful, I am certainly barking up the wrong tree. I wake up from my dreams drenched in sweat. Is it possible? This man, a celebrated child analyst, a professor of Psychiatry at Stanford University, is missing something crucial in the analysis, of which I myself am aware? Should I believe the analyst, surrender my authority to his, take comfort in having him know me better than I know myself? How can I know that I am caught up in a grand moment of self-evolution, which seems to have become sufficiently disturbing to him that he cannot let it unfold through its own wild, exuberant declarations?

This man, to whom for eight years I have turned in every desperate situation, seems someone on whom I can presently not rely. At times, this seems terrifying. It threatens to awaken the specter of self-disintegration, to call up another episode in the old epic of the dismembered self, the bad nights, the mounting anxiety, the danger of sprawling into fragments.

One late afternoon as I am walking down the stairs after our session I feel that something has violently snapped in my relations to him. He, who for these many years has lived inside me as a protective presence, has just been dislodged from that role. Something tells me I will never be able to trust him again. This experience ought to be shattering. I stand at the bottom of the stairs, gazing at the street, expecting it to take on an alien appearance, as the known world falls away from me, to leave me skinless, exposed. But as I get into my car the loss of the analytic-protector takes on an oddly settled shape, becoming a defined internal event that can be lived with. I am negotiating the heavy traffic, I am all of a piece, I have held together.

During the next session, as I am telling him about this loss of trust, which the analyst (seems to) understand as a last fling with regression before the analysis legitimately comes to an end, the analyst suddenly loses his authority. It removes itself from him. I no longer believe he knows what is happening between us.

I explain my dilemma. Whether or not I am right in my perception of his anger, I would have to tell him about this perception. That is how analysis works. But my attempts to tell him sound like challenges to him; my challenges have come to be seen as acts of aggression, thus convincing the analyst that the anger is mine, not his.

Meanwhile, I am aware that my version of things is a subjective account, biased, highly inflected. Perhaps it is I who am blind, don't understand what is happening, am spinning out a transferential epic because I don't know how else to bring our relationship to an end?

The analyst probably believes I need my anger in order to leave him. He might be right. He believes my anger comes from the past. No doubt I have also been angry at my father. Perhaps indeed I have confused the analyst's playful opinions with my father's Marxism, which (the analyst again points out) could never be discussed in jest.

It does not occur to either of us that I, after twenty-five years, may be freeing myself from a need for an organizing ideology. No analyst has ever suggested that I have been loyal to psychoanalysis because I have been (unconsciously) working out an attachment to fundamental "objective" truths, whether Marxist or Freudian. If an analyst had wondered whether psychoanalysis had anything to offer me, especially after so many years of interpretive work, he would have had to ask whether the psychoanalytic world-view had caught and held on to me, not only because it was useful, helpful, healing, but because it offered a replacement for the dogmatic structure I had lost when I gave up the Marxist faith of my childhood. Perhaps, over all the analytic years, my symptoms had changed form, persisted, gone away, come back again, in order to keep me loyal to the ideological structure of a world-explaining truth, while yet allowing me to express hostility toward that truth for failing me. As interpretations go, that would have been nifty, it might even have been liberating, but it was never made. Indeed, the analyst apparently has not noticed that I have just gone through another wholesale reworking of my self. He does not seem to realize the transformation has finally, after an analytic lifetime of struggle toward this end, taken place without disintegration. What he regards as challenge, anger, aggression against his authority, the reliving of a traumatic paternal past, I experience as the coming to life of a new organization of myself, which he is aborting.

Whose version are we to believe?

I make several appointments to consult with other analysts about my analytic situation. One of the consultants, who has been practicing as an analyst for some fifty years, can imagine that I, who am highly sensitive to anger, may be aware of an anger the analyst disowns. She wonders, however, whether there is really such an imperative need to keep trying to convince him. She imagines I can claim my own authority for this experience of him, whether or not he shares my view.

I dream that I have stormed out of an analytic session.

The third analyst seems not to take seriously the threatening messages of the dreams. He doesn't seem to know that the analysis is becoming unbearable because of this strange warfare in which both of us participate, although he does not own up to his part.

I come to every session resolved to get to the bottom of things analytically. He too seems resolved to set out on a positive note. I can feel his good will, the effort to meet me halfway. We start out quietly musing in an analytic vein. Ten, fifteen minutes into the session, the heat is on, my voice is rising, his is getting tighter, colder, more controlled.

Sometimes I think, if only he would admit that he is angry. Through this anger he would have met me person to person in the most radical psychoanalytic space. Sometimes I think, if only he would admit that he is in conflict. In his conflict between the old authority and the analyst's new ability to let down his hair, he is as fully human as I am, flawed, imperfect, struggling, caught between what he has been until this moment, what he is becoming even now, perhaps in this very trouble with me. Here he is, impatient, challenged, meeting up with me human to human just as I wish to be met, but he cannot know it and he cannot admit it and therefore, even as it is happening between us, the encounter cannot take place.

On the way to one of the last sessions, I find myself thinking about an old Zen story. During the next weeks I become obsessed with this story. I tell it to my lover, repeat it to my friends over coffee, go over it silently with myself.

The disciple, after some twenty, thirty years of study,

knowing he is ready to become a master in his own right, goes up to the master one morning and breaks the master's staff.

In the Zen tradition this is appropriate etiquette. By breaking the staff, the disciple has declared himself independent, ready to set off on his own. His discipleship has ended. But it is difficult to tell this story in an analytic context. I am afraid the staff might get translated into a phallic symbol, the anecdote itself heard as a tale of penis envy. In that form, it would be difficult to hear it as a Zen story, celebrating the legitimate break between master and disciple.

Evidently, tales that cannot be told must be enacted. Because psychoanalysis does not have a comparable traditional gesture, my analyst has undoubtedly perceived my staff-breaking as an act of aggression. In my version of things, I am becoming my self through a gesture of theoretical independence. Since it does not seem possible to discover the truth of the situation (which can only be approximated through these differing versions of what is taking place), I will have to rely on my own version.

I have already ceased to experience the analyst as a protective presence. The authority for understanding what is happening between us has shifted from him to me. I have given up the effort to define the "truth" of our interaction or make him capable of grasping mine. I am not going to surrender my sense of what is happening. I am going to break the analyst's staff.

*   *   *

My memory! A highly subjective, tendentious, self-serving ground, which has already put a spin on events it appears simply to have recorded. Granted, I am a hothead. I am also stubborn. When I make up my mind, sooner or later I will go my own way. That is what twenty-five years of analysis have accomplished. I have never felt the third analyst appreciated these rebellious qualities in me. On the other hand, I am about to set off on the road alone. Therefore, I will be lucky to have these traits. My cunning, sharp-eyed, streetwise, work-things-out-for-myself attitude will no doubt also be a valuable possession. But if I am leaving, I want my twenty-five years of analytic work to have a suitable end.

Therefore, I am going to try yet again, in a calm voice, restraining my excitement, to tell the analyst how I am planning to work as an analytic listener, now that I have come to believe a different kind of listening is necessary, if we are to hear our analysands into their own voices.

The analyst does not see much in this different kind of listening. It sounds to him like the listening he and many other analysts already do. This is a tough moment. If I say, But there really is something distinctive about this type of listening, will he feel that I am aggressively pointing to his limitations? If I have something new in mind, does this imply that he is limited? Do I think he is limited? A dilemma. Can I have a new idea without doing violence to him?

We are arguing. It is an argument about listening. I believe that when interpretations are being made, the analyst is no longer listening. If the analyst interprets, the analyst is robbing the analysand of her voice. This new listening I have in mind is not the same as empathic listening, reflective listening, intersubjective listening, hermeneutic listening, social-constructivist listening (the new, fashionable listenings in psychoanalysis). For one thing, the listener is no longer an authority. The kind of analytic listener I have in mind is actively engaged in learning the distinctive language of another's self-expression. Usually, we assume another person is speaking our language because we use the same words. In fact, within the common language, everyone is subtly speaking her own. This type of different listening has something in common with the learning of a foreign language, in which you must put aside your own linguistic habits to enter a new and distinctive linguistic mode. This listening also has something in common with a child's rapt listening to bedtime stories. It is the sort of listening that gives rise to the ancient art of oral storytelling. When the analyst manages to listen in this way, unheard voices of the other's self begin to find language. Finding one's own voice. Telling one's own story. That is the sort of psychoanalysis I would like to offer to people who come to speak with me.

These things are not spoken in a calm voice. They are meeting (I believe) with opposition. They are becoming strident. I am talking too fast, the way I do. I am interrupting the analyst, who is interrupting me. I seem determined to have my say. He too seems determined.

Is it possible to listen without preconception? Is one doomed to organize another's experience according to one's own worldview? If so, what happens to the listening when the listener is fully aware of her bias? Might she not, at least for a moment or two, be able to peek around the corner of her own temperament, to catch something unique, unexpected in the personality of the other? If a full disclosure about bias and worldview are made, isn't the storyteller then freed to set aside the authority the listener might otherwise carry?

We are some halfway through the session. We have been debating these issues with tremendous heat. It is clear to me that I am not the only person who has grown excited. Perhaps the analyst is letting himself go, stepping out of his strict analytic role to participate in a fiery engagement? That's what I might do when I thought a client had become sturdy enough to experiment with disagreement. But somehow, I have the impression the analyst does not know he too is hot under the collar. I have the feeling he thinks I am the only person who has grown excited.

There is a momentary pause. I am trying to gather my

thoughts for the next round of disputation. The analyst says: "You argue too well."

This is a stunning statement. Too well? Does that mean he can't win the argument with me, settle it definitively with an authoritative pronouncement? Does it mean I won't give up my own point of view? How can someone argue too well?

My thoughts move fast. They divide against themselves, they try to restore him to his superior knowing. Perhaps arguing too well means that I can't listen to what he is trying to tell me? Perhaps it means I am defending myself against feeling? Perhaps I am displacing, projecting, transferring, acting out, avoiding, projectively identifying, flying out against internalized, negative objects?

Now it is I who am trying to keep my voice steady. "I argue as well as I must to get my point across."

The analyst has just disappeared. I don't have to look around to know he is no longer present. However sturdily he keeps to his chair, he has just vanished. His silence marks a retreat, a disappearing act, a vanishing.

I am still struggling with my voice, its high-pitched, urgent notes. "I would like to *know* what you mean when *you* say I argue too well."

From a lofty distance, with only the very slightest hint of arrogance, he says, "Why don't you just lie back and think about it."

Is he kidding? Lie back and think about it? Dutifully, obediently, muse on his words? I think the analyst is in

deep trouble. He is trying to establish an analytic authority he himself has long since theoretically disavowed. We
are slipping back out of our radically revisionist psychoanalysis, with its deconstructed, subtle awareness of subjective states, into a century-old authoritarianism. The
analyst is trying to pull rank on me.

"Well," I say, surprised at my own sudden calm, "I'd
like to know what you have on your mind. If you have
something to say, why don't you just say it?"

A brief silence. Then he says, as if after weighty con-
sideration, "I have nothing further to say."

He has nothing further to say. "Well then, neither do I."

Endings come fast, they tumble over their own heels,
they are a downhill business. I gather up my sweater,
stand up, walk deliberately to the door. The dream, in
which I had walked out of an analytic session, is coming
true. I have just broken the master's staff.

At the door, I turn back to look at him. This will be
the last time.

"I am saying good-bye. And I mean good-bye."

He nods, taking in the implication.

Twenty-five years of analysis have just come to an
end.

Time for an interpretation. How do I know? I've been
reading over my last sections. I see that they have
descended linguistically to the level of a street brawl. The
old man once said to me, "Interpretations have their

place. They are very soothing to the analyst." I too have often found interpretations useful, they have a way of wrapping things up, help you believe explanations are possible, truth can be known, insights have power over unreason. Just now I noticed how raw and rough my writing had become, lacking polish, urbane distance. What better time to shuffle out an interpretation.

Once you get used to this type of thought you can dance around in analytic double toe loops, gracefully. This will help produce a virtuoso performance, which one may or may not subsequently take seriously, depending on one's need for explanations. For my purposes, here, an explanation is essential; it will serve to reestablish the appropriate tone, which my raw anger has disrupted.

Deliberately, then, with a willed return to formality, I look back over my analytic years. I am mindful of that buried structure I have observed before: a symptom that brings me into analysis, a self-experience that is generated by the analysis, only to be left out of each until a subsequent eruption of feeling disorders the analysis and leads to departure.

In the first analysis, the yearning of self for self, which came to be focused on the analyst, could not be adequately met through ideas of will, self-discipline, transference. Therefore, the perilous phenomenology of the self, winding along from obsession, through yearning, to breakdown, could not be contained within the analytic vessel. The yearning was cast out into a shadow analysis, from which it erupted in those attacks of panic that brought the analysis to an end.

In the second analysis, the self's research could not enter the analytic discourse, which tended to give premature cognitive form to prelinguistic raptures. But if the self's story could not be told, the self would not be able to take the analyst as an object of desire, the loved one who listens, the beloved who has heard. Therefore, in the second analysis, the transference through desire could not be engaged, an object outside the analysis had to be found. Inevitably, the self found the woman from New England, who was (as it happens) also an analyst. She had to be there to organize the force of desire that had emerged in the name of bisexuality. Because she was outside the analytic work, the desire for her disrupted the analysis, leading once again to departure.

In the third analysis, it was my evolution as a psychoanalytic listener that could not easily enter the analysis. My consultation work with the old man, my growing sense of analytic self-authority, my proud, fitful knowledge of a new way to listen to another's tale became the shadow to the analytic work, the potentially disruptive absence that could not bring itself into the analytic sessions. The third analyst, who had been so remarkable a listener to the troubled, prelinguistic child, had not been able to hear the self-celebrations of the woman. The woman growing up, the woman coming into her own, the woman finding her own voice, had become the force erupting out of shadow, to disrupt the analysis, to bring about departure.

If these interpretations flatten my story, I cannot be blamed. Flattening is a bosom friend to interpretation. When you are very upset, when you can't make sense of something, when you meet with all your friends to discuss your turmoil, there will be interpretation. The habit of it, the need for it, does not end with analysis. The friend with whom I discuss psychoanalysis had his own interpretation of my psychoanalytic ending. He thought the analyst himself had changed over the years I had been with him, during which he had become a celebrated researcher with a devoted following. My friend thought the third analyst may have begun to take pleasure in the way other people deferred to his analytic authority, therefore deeply resenting my (disrespectful) challenges. My friend also thought I may have enjoyed my power to discredit the analyst as a clinician, by making my own analysis with him considerably less than a therapeutic triumph.

Another friend, a professor of literature, thought that I may have provoked the theoretical disputes with the analyst to prove to myself that he would not be destroyed by my power. We still haven't been able to determine whether the third analyst should be said, symbolically speaking, to have gone under because of my departure or to have survived. During another discussion my friend came up with the astonishing idea that the old man had displaced the analyst as a father figure, a dislocation in the symbolic realm that brought about a significant change in the analysis. Once he had been deposed as father, the analyst and I (she felt) had fallen into a rivalry over the question of lineage and inheritance. She read the caviar dream (should the caviar be eaten with feta or sour cream?) as evidence for this sibling struggle.

Another friend was sure the analysis was not over, that the analyst would contact me, the work would go on. My friend had known me make dramatic gestures before now. He reminded me I was likely, as time passed, to make an equally dramatic turnabout back into the analysis.

My partner found the ending entirely appropriate, in keeping with the passionate way I did most things. Therefore, she felt, my analysis should end as it had, dramatically. She also thought the third analyst had been wonderful at receiving a small child, but like many fathers, could not maintain a relationship with a daughter as she became a woman.

Another friend, who did not think highly of analysts in general, had come to the conclusion that I had been conducting my own analysis for years, while consistently handing over my authority to my analysts.

A colleague, with whom I met regularly to discuss clinical issues, thought that I had been caught in a conflict of loyalty between two fathers, one of whom kept a vigilant distance, the other of whom, because we were colleagues, invited me warmly into his life, introduced me to his wife, invited me for coffee, went out to lunch with me and my partner.

Another colleague thought a primitive vulnerability had been touched in both me and the analyst, becoming explosive because we had both been in too much pain to give the vulnerability a name.

I myself was impressed that, during the several months of troubled ending, I had not imagined the analysis to have split apart into two analyses, an early good analysis, followed by a later bad analysis, in which the seemingly good analyst of the beginning was replaced by a bad analyst, who had now revealed his true nature. Even during spells of strenuous anger I never seemed to forget how he had been there to receive a little child whose story had not been able to find language before.

My German tutor had a typically eccentric view, partly in humor and in large part, I felt, seriously. When I first told him about the arguments between me and the third analyst, he said, "He's having trouble letting you go. I think he's fallen for you. Nothing wrong with that. So have I."

"You and I are a different matter," I said. "We enjoy being in love with each other."

"That's true," he replied.

In the silence that followed, I watched the long spiral down of a eucalyptus leaf outside the window. On another day, when I was very upset, the German tutor said: "If I were an analyst I would say, 'Well, we've done a good piece of work. We like to talk together. Why don't we wrap this up and have coffee?'"

"That will never happen," I replied.

"No," he said, with a somewhat weary gesture, "I suppose not."

These ideas make up a wholesome interpretive feast, although none swallows up the mystery of the ending. This mystery reminds me of the self-replenishing bowl of milk, the ever-renewing loaf of bread left behind for their hosts by the gods who had visited them disguised as mortals. Because I entertained psychoanalysis for all those years, I have taken away with me a self-renewing mystery. Therefore, it seems, I will never go hungry again.

Of course, it could be said that with all this hidden structure, shadowy exclusion, eruption, departure, father conflict, sibling struggle, I successfully resisted psychoanalysis over twenty-five years. Or perhaps it would be equally true to say that, during those same twenty-five years, psychoanalysis successfully resisted me?

Epilogue

A Termination

(1992)

I am in the woods. There is a tree that branches fairly close to the ground. Because of this branching it is easy to climb up into the tree. From my perch I look down into a grove of oaks covered in moss and lichen. This is the place I come when I have things to think over.

Today is the day after I have walked out of the analytic session. Because I have spent the evening with my friend Lillian, telling her about this break with my analyst, today I am calm. This calm seems menacing. I don't believe in it. I am sure it will not last. Sooner or later (I fear sooner) it will break down into the old anxiety. I will be brought to my knees. I will have to go crawling back to the analyst. But I will not go! Therefore, I am likely to be in trouble.

I wait. The calm grows larger. Out of it an analytic monologue begins to unfold. I listen to it as if I were hearing a distinct but distant voice. As I listen, my calm gives way to a considerable excitement. I have just heard the unintimidated voice of the self. When I get home, I jot down its words. Within a few hours they have become a letter to the analyst.

I am writing to confirm that I will not be keeping my regular hour on Monday, and won't be expecting you to hold it open for me. Although certainly not a conventional termination, we do seem to be at the end of a long, successful process. I had imagined something very different, but I do not find this particular ending as troubling as I might have expected. Indeed, there even seems to be something strangely appropriate about it, since I feel that what I have to say about psychoanalysis cannot really be said within the psychoanalytic process. Over the last three and a half months I have come to feel this more and more definitely, and therefore, for us both to end with the statement "I have nothing further to say," is perhaps simply exactly right. In any case, such as it is, I can live with this ending.

I think the quality of our work together over the last seven or eight years has been exceptional; the last three months do not seem to have been at the same level, but that certainly does not change my sense of the depth, meaning, significance, worth of the work itself. Perhaps, later on, the explanation for this particular ending will occur to one or both of us. I myself, at this moment, find much to be grateful for, much to be proud of, much to smile about.

In that sense, not a bad ending, after all.

Thank you.

I may have waited a day or two before mailing the letter. On the other hand, I wanted it to arrive on time to free up the Monday session. I thought the analyst would know better than to take the letter at face value. I am bringing our dialogue to a close. Truth, fully told, would be an invitation to discourse. Ours is over.

I am on the way to the mailbox. Am I really going to mail this letter? Can a piece of paper bring twenty-five years of analysis to an end? I am opening the slot, placing the letter, letting it fall down irretrievably into the box.

As I walk home, I take the opportunity to kick up a rumpus in a pile of brittle leaves.

During the next week a bill arrives, including a charge for our last session. With it, there is a note from the analyst wishing me well. When I read this note, I believe the analyst is sincere in his wishes.

I staple his note to my letter, put both of them away in my special letter file. I want to preserve an accurate record of this ending.

A day or two later I return to the woods. Back in the tree, looking down through a misty, early-morning light at the druidical landscape, the still, small voice shows up again. This time it pieces together a monologue I will never send to the third analyst, although it is addressed to him. It goes something like this:

I have thought it might be possible to keep a small corner of psychoanalysis open for the potential outsiders. I imagined it a psychoanalytic outpost, the house at the end of the road, the cottage closest to the woods. A place where people come by to speak about things not usually mentioned elsewhere. There is an elderly woman with whom they come to speak. She is perhaps an image of my future.

Her psychoanalysis is no longer a therapeutic methodology, if therapy means a treatment for people who are ill, who wish to consult an authority to find out what is wrong with them. She is a person with the capacity to draw out the life story of another, while refraining from giving that story a shape. She also does not claim to know. She can recognize a good story when she has heard one, knows when a story is going wrong, evading something, skimming the surface, snaking around to avoid crucial details, missing a center, rambling, not getting to the point, getting too consistently to the point, not having learned the virtue of detour, byway, coloration. She is a practitioner of listening. That means wide-eyed, eager to hear more, exuberant, downcast, excited when the story calls upon those responses, curious to know where the story is going, which makes it possible for a story to go on.

Listening in this way, without spinning an interpretive pattern for another's tale, seems to her a useful approach for artists, other creative people, folk with a mystical bent, the outsiders who wish to endure their condition (although it can be tough going), who have no wish to take to the more well-trodden path or for those insiders who might have strayed onto it and want some help getting back off. It is an approach likely to appeal to anyone in self-pursuit of herself, whose trouble might follow her, as mine followed me, both day and night, alone, together with others, bringing her face to face with all those obscure, troubling conditions of the self about which I had been learning during the last twenty-five years.

This approach does not seem to be therapy (a treatment for someone who is ill), because it holds that anyone capable of pursuing a self is to be counted among the sturdier members of the species. It is not an interpretive psychoanalysis, because it holds that anyone capable of telling her own story will know what to make of it. This art, which shifts the narrative responsibility to the client, depends upon an odd mix of engagement and withholding. Stretching oneself out to enter the world of another. Holding oneself back to let the other fill the interpretive space the analyst's listening has made possible. It respects the shaping power of childhood experience, is interested in the workings of memory, helps create the interior space in which transformations of the self take place. For those reasons, although occupying a remote corner, it has remained psychoanalysis.

It is possible that my path to that elder woman has led legitimately through graduate school and formal study. It is, however, equally possible: those formal years have been a long detour, delaying my arrival at the place to which I had always been heading, on this obscure, erratic, ruthless, determined, unfocused, highly disciplined leap in the direction of the self.

Words of this sort are never written down. They are

scratched on a piece of bark, then forgotten, until they emerge, in some form or another, to close a story. With them, my twenty-five years as an analytic patient rounded themselves out. The third analyst might never hear me. Today I had said what I had to say.

A story that might have had many versions can also not have a definitive end. One of these days I will sit down to describe in detail my work with the old man, who, by radically telling his own stories, deconstructed psychoanalysis for me. (He would have grinned mysteriously in the presence of the word "deconstruction.") Perhaps I will suddenly be able to tell about the way I have painstakingly learned to listen over the years to those who have come to work with me. With them, I have figured out how to provide a different type of analytic environment, in which they can repeat Freud's original act of self-discovery, without being translated into Freud. But for that story still to come the narrative gaze will have to turn from me to those from whom I have been learning. It is, it seems, a story that will require time to prepare itself, through selective acts of memory and forgetting. For now, I have said what I have to say. I am falling silent.

I might have known. How could I possibly hope to pack twenty-five years of analytic experience on both sides of the couch into a single book? Knowledge of this sort, full of chagrin at its own prior audacity, is the suitable ending to a book, not its appropriate beginning. If the psychoanalysis of the self cannot end before the self itself, how could a book about psychoanalysis hope to achieve a settled closure? Next year's harvest of acorns, still latent, along with what has yet to unfold, must necessarily clutter a psychoanalytic ending. For this tale of the three analyses, the only possible end is therefore an abrupt, not fully rounded, almost-legitimate, unexpected termination.

Not so fast! This is an epilogue, it is entitled to ramble, grow contemporary, make bold claims, celebrate the completion of a difficult project. Recently, I have been following the psychoanalytic wars in the national press, rumors about the death of Freud, revelations about his unknown nature. All this is of great interest to me. If Freud is dead, where does that leave me, who have just spent twenty-five years of my life in his shadow? Clearly, this is not a question I can evade on behalf of a cut-throat ending.

In response to an article on Freud by a well-known professor of English, Frederick Crews, a celebrated anti-Freudian, *The New York Review of Books* has recently been flooded with mail from psychoanalysts. They object to Crews's "misunderstandings" and "scurrilous" comments, his article's seemingly angry voice, his "misreadings" and "misrepresentations," "polemical flourishes," "selective" and "misleading" emphases. It is true, the article about the Unknown Freud was not written calmly.

Nevertheless, I also agree with most of the points it makes, although I cannot seem to follow them to the writer's conclusion. Frederick Crews is concerned with the unscientific nature of Freud's work, the flawed texture of his inferential paths, his inadequate assessment of the effect upon patients of psychoanalytic suggestion, the lack of first-generation therapeutic success that would justify Freud's pride in psychoanalysis, a wild interpretive psychoanalytic self-permissiveness, the invention of unwarranted theory to buttress failed earlier stages of theoretical speculation, the dogmatic nature of psychoanalysis, its institutional investment in upholding its truth claims. I can agree with these things, they tally in many respects with features of my own psychoanalytic experience. Therefore, where does that leave me? Caught somewhere between Freud's militant detractors and most impassioned defenders? An outsider again? That's okay. I'm getting used to it.

Trouble is, I can't really see what all the fuss is about. Who cares if psychoanalysis is scientific? It doesn't even upset me much when someone offers up Freud as a cocaine addict, semidelirious, a borderline psychotic, making grandiose, self-serving truth claims on the basis of his self-analysis. This Freud, ruled by demons, is precisely the Freud who has always appealed to me.

I can't imagine how a message from the underworld could have been brought back by a scientific search party that does not recognize its existence. For me, Freud is western culture's most dramatic shaman, repeating the great archaic journey to other worlds in his own staid Victorian person. I guess it is a pity he felt constrained to translate his wild, somber gleanings into the scientific currency of his day. But I can understand this too. He must have been looking for a cage in which to trap his demons, some rigorous, cognitive act of definition that would forever confine them. Of course he failed, the underworld prefers poets and their evocations, it is a bit too slippery for theoretical proclamations, and right there my Faustian Freud takes on his enduring fascination. What an undertaking! What a magnificent failure! This unheard-of attempt to make science out of human passions. I have managed (even after all my years of psychoanalysis) to remain sufficiently romantic to cherish Freud as a somewhat tragic figure. A twentieth-century Dante, let us say, forced by paternal and professional obligations, the need to earn a living, an ambitious desire for recognition, to write our century's divine comedy in the cool, seemingly reasonable language of science.

But what about the stench of sulfur that rises from Freud's work? Because of this potent underworld emission, in which Freud's work is drenched, in spite of its efforts at science, one cannot stop reading him. I know, I have tried.

As it happens, my own reading of Freud began a year before my analysis with the fair-spoken analyst I loved in my youth. I was introduced to Freud by a brilliant young professor of English. He taught Shakespeare to us as if the great bard had been reading Freud. Through Hamlet, in the young professor's reading of him, I first found out about forbidden sexual desire for one's mother, the repressed wish to slay one's father, the paralyzing guilt that might arise (merely) from having wished to kill the man—especially when one's uncle had just dispatched him.

That was almost thirty years ago now. I suppose, with only a little exaggeration, I could blame my entire career as a psychoanalytic patient on that slender young professor, who stood tall, spoke well, made such beautiful gestures while initiating his rapt adolescent audience into the unknown mysteries of literary psychoanalysis. Perhaps an attentive reader will have guessed his name by now?

I don't know if I believe in transference. I certainly believe in meeting the right teacher at the right time, falling for what he has to say, never forgetting him, tracing back one's intellectual lineage to his lectures. Right back through all those rising and falling selves of the last three decades, I can still detect the seedlings of my psychoanalytic self in that young woman who sat in the back row of a lecture room in Wheeler Hall, while Frederick Crews held forth to his eager students.

Because of this early history, its lasting influence, the somewhat transferential quality of my attachment to my teacher, I am puzzled. Why is he still so outraged at

Freud when I have forgiven him? Was he once a psycho-analytic patient too, a believer in psychoanalytic claims to hold a truth that holds a healing power? (Anyone who has been analyzed would probably make that interpreta-tion. Therefore, one must immediately suspect it.) Cer-tainly, it is very disappointing when psychoanalysis fails to justify this claim. It could even set off decades of ruthless-ness. And that's good. A ruthless impatience about truth is a powerful inspiration, likely to provoke a life's work, catch it on fire, heat up its brilliance, make it unresting. I admire my former teacher for his raids against psychoanal-ysis. As for myself, I must have stopped believing in psy-choanalysis a long time ago. I think I hung around after that because I had taken to Freud's habit of peering into himself. When other people have tried to translate me into Freud, I resisted. This has made for a stormy, irregular psy-choanalytic experience, but why should I blame Freud for that? I have my own underworld, as useful to me as Freud's proved to be for him.

If Freud, in time, should come to be seen as nothing more than an eloquent twentieth-century popularizer of the archaic underworld (the id, the unconscious), I might still be content to have lived so many formative years in his shadow.

Is this an apology for Freud? Hardly.

I dream: I am climbing an immense ladder that stretches out from the center of the world far into the heavens.

As I climb, I look down, terrified by how high I am, how fatal, therefore, a slip, a fall. When I look up, I am equally terrified by how far I still have to go. Nevertheless, I keep climbing. Soon I come to the last houses at the top of the world, where carpenters are at work on the rooftops. My ladder has come to an end. Out beyond the houses there is a muddy, slippery slope. I get off my ladder and start scrambling up, sliding, falling back, going forward. But suddenly I remember the ladder, turn back, get my hands on it, drag it along with me.

This dream occurred more than once during the first analysis, where it was interpreted as my willingness to take reason (the ladder) along with me into the unknown. The dream has also occurred several times since then. Recently, a psychoanalytic friend, over coffee in a crowded café, offered his interpretation of the dream. He saw the ladder as a symbol for psychoanalysis, which I have outgrown but can't leave behind. The waiter interrupted us to serve the coffee.

Why do I still think of the work I do as psychoanalytic? Psychoanalysis, with its flaws, grandiosities, misguided claims, its need to examine its first principles, its high expectations for itself, its inevitable disappointments, reminds me a bit of what I have learned from psychoanalysis about myself. Then too, I don't know much about anything else, except writing. Even my writing has always been submerged in analytic waters. I remain Jewish while I deplore the behavior of fundamentalist Jews

210

in Crown Heights or the West Bank. I remain a woman, in spite of the frequent self-betrayal of women. I am incorrigibly given to self-reflection, fascinated by the inner worlds of others, curious about what psychoanalysis might become when it stops trying to make itself a science. If the dream says I climbed off the psychoanalytic ladder, it also says I am determined to take psychoanalysis along with me. A grandiose interpretation? Even my grandiosity has survived twenty-five psychoanalytic years.

What's that, a happy ending? The troubled young woman spends twenty-five years in analysis, endures the life and death of the self until a stable configuration is achieved, consolidates this accomplishment by breaking with the third analyst, thereby giving up the need for ideology, a definitive worldview, truth, a preordained authority, in favor of an ambiguous, creative relationship to a perpetually evolving self?

But what about those things that have been left out of the story? Did everything neatly tie itself up the minute the letter to the analyst was mailed? What about the heartbreak, the sense of loss, the betrayal, the anger breaking through, the rough edge, the unfinished?

I had gone to see a film. (This is a dream.) The ticket seemed very expensive but I paid it anyway. When I got inside, and talked with my partner, it turned out that I had been greatly overcharged. I decided to go back to complain. My partner said, "Well, take it easy; keep things calm." I went back to the box office. "Give me back my money," I stormed. The ticket seller, a young woman, was smoking a cigar. There was a small burning stub of cigar on the table next to her. I grabbed it.

One might not, apart from the cigar, associate this dream with psychoanalysis: my rage for having been cheated, charged too much. But the young girl smoking a cigar, that's the giveaway. The ticket seller is a dream image for the psychoanalyst, maybe even for Freud himself, a habitual cigar man. This is a dream with a sense of humor.

On the other hand: why was the cigar-smoking, ticket-selling analyst a young girl? Could she have been an image of me? The girl who received the icon? The girl in the turtleneck sweater? The young nun, perhaps? Was it the splinter woman getting out of her car to cross the street to the first analyst? Perhaps (says the dream) it was all of them together who charged too much for my analysis?

Goodness knows what we are to make of this dream with a sense of humor. Could it be trying to suggest I usurped the role of analyst (got hold of the cigar) when still a young girl, so that I have only myself to blame for cheating myself, charging myself too much, handing over authority while secretly, silently, through all those years, planning to steal that cigar-laden authority for myself?

How long ago was it that I ended my twenty-five

years of analysis? A year and a half ago? Long enough, I admit, to test the self's capacity to keep itself together. Therefore, the psychoanalysis has succeeded, a coherent self has been forged out of warring fragments. So where's the quarrel? Who got cheated? Why the need to storm off with the cigar?

My original experiment has come to an end. I have produced an analysis of my psychoanalysis, writing spontaneously, fast as I could, without censoring or clipping back. Because I have been following a theme, I have necessarily left out everything that does not contribute to the thematic discharge. A true story, it has its limitations. It is a version fully aware that other versions might have been told.

I have never yet written a book that worked out the way I planned. Didn't I say so from the beginning? Nevertheless, before we part company, I had better subject that triptych to one final bit of scrutiny. What's it driving at? Why is it still sitting around above my desk? Why do I drag it with me all over the world? The icon must be hundreds of years old by now. I myself have cherished it for thirty-five. Will my daughter get it after I'm gone? If it has become a family heirloom, what's that supposed to mean? As a family, we've had our fling with Marxism (a materialist worldview). I've put in my time with psychoanalysis (skeptical, scientific). Don't tell me there's some mystical leaning we can't quite get rid of, some yearning for wholeness, union, perhaps even a belief in them, that has come along with us all the way through Marxism and psychoanalysis, postmodernism, deconstruction? Perhaps my self has been unfolding as steadily, inevitably as a blade of grass from grass seed. Maybe I have become what I was always meant to be, this message impressed on every particle of self-potential.

This yearning, with its fierce mystical tonality, never got a good hearing (so far as I know) in either Marxism or psychoanalysis. Therefore, it may be that my quest for wholeness has come to feel forbidden, stolen, as if it were contraband goods. Maybe that's why it has to be represented by the complex figure of a Jew, a nonbeliever, carting around a stolen Christian icon.

Did I just say I was a nonbeliever?

I've already demonstrated my incompatibility with science. If I am a nonbeliever, that is only because I don't like other people's giving names to what I believe. This is the spirit, I suppose, in which I stole the cigar. With the dream cigar I may have taken to myself Freud's original power for naming his own experience. Freud, the only psychoanalyst who was never analyzed.

When Freud wanted to understand himself he sought counsel from his own dreams. After Freud no one has repeated this original act of psychoanalysis. After Freud, we've used his names, borrowed the stories he liked to tell. Is that the sense in which I have been letting myself be charged too much? Freud picked out Oedipus from among a thousand mythical faces because Oedipus had in common with Freud an abiding love for his mother, a bitter quarrel with his father. Now that I have got hold of Freud's cigar, I may be able to accomplish (whether triptych or trilogy) my own design. Maybe, with that cigar in my hands, I will be able to describe the different kind of listening I practice, from which a long story remains to be made.